Winnipesaukee C

MW00758283

HUNGRY FOR SUMMER

A Unique Collection of Favorite Recipes
from the
Island Residents of Lake Winnipesaukee

Jeannette Buell and Daryl Thompson

Outskirts Press, Inc.
Denver, Colorado

Winnipesaukee Cuisine presents Hungry for Summer - A Unique Collection of Favorite Recipes from the Island Residents of Lake Winnipesaukee
All Rights Reserved.
Copyright © 2010 Jeannette Buell & Daryl Thompson
V3.0 R2.0

Outskirts Press, Inc.
http://www.outskirtspress.com

ISBN: 978-1-4327-1185-6

Outskirts Press and the "OP" logo are trademarks belonging to Outskirts Press, Inc.

PRINTED IN THE UNITED STATES OF AMERICA

Cover Photograph: Rock Island, Gilford, New Hampshire
Courtesy of the Carbone Family

This book is a compilation of favorite, tried-and-true recipes representing the culinary lifestyle of the island residents of Lake Winnipesaukee.

The origin of the recipes is unknown to us unless otherwise stated. All recipes have been tested to ensure accuracy. Some recipes may include minor changes or suggested additions that the testers felt necessary for the most successful outcome.

The stories have been edited for grammar and some have been compressed to fit within the confines of this book's layout. Every effort has been made to keep the integrity of the material that was submitted for this project.

Due to our publishing restraints, not all submitted materials could be printed, but credit has been given to all who contributed.

We would like to express our heartfelt gratitude to all of you who were so willing to share your history, hijinx, traditions and recipes with us.

COOKING IS LIKE LOVE.
IT SHOULD BE ENTERED INTO WITH ABANDON OR NOT AT ALL.
Harriet Van Horne

Lake Winnipesaukee
Smile of the Great Spirit

What is it like living on an island on Lake Winnipesaukee?

Hungry for Summer offers a glimpse into island life through the shared recipes, stories and photographs of fellow islanders.

With this book we hope to take you on a cruise, navigating the lake from island to island, sharing what is, for us, the most beautiful place on earth... each summer day, another day in paradise.

What is it like, this unique lifestyle? It's time spent with family and friends; it's a different sunrise or sunset everyday; it's the wildlife that entertain us; it's the fruit of the land...blueberries. It's a common bond islanders share with each other. It's a treasure we share with you.

Acknowledgments

Our heart-felt gratitude to our families for their patience and support throughout this project. They lived with us in our often single-focused, distracted and deadline-driven state for a very long time. Special thanks to our husbands: to Bill Buell for so much, but especially for the months spent kitchen-testing and sampling recipes, and for the days spent navigating the lake, helping to deliver our printed materials from island-to-island and dock-to-dock. The places we saw and the people we met made those days very special, bringing to light a new appreciation of just how vast and diversely beautiful our lake is.

And...to Brad Thompson for his knowledge of the lake, his many good suggestions, and especially for sharing the lobster-bake secrets of his salty old buddy, Seaweed Steve, and recording them for history, with words and illustration.

To our many friends for their support and for enduring the highs and lows: to Barbara Lauterbach – teacher, author, friend and mentor, for sharing her invaluable experience and knowledge, and for being our biggest cheerleader. To Sue Cutillo - friend and mentor, for having faith in us from the very beginning. Her insight and her endless enthusiasm for our project were invaluable. To Dale Dormody – website designer, for getting us headed in the right direction with our website and giving us the tools necessary to figure things out. To Sally Keroack, Pam Seed and Brenda Keith for their magnifying-glass editing skills. To Jill Billings Buell - for being our photography-go-to-expert.

To Brenda Keith- for coming up with the title, *Hungry for Summer*. To Joe Fagnant - for catching the elusive lake trout needed for the recipe-testing.

And finally, to all of our recipe-testers without whom we'd still be cooking: Kim and Mary Anne Baron, Judy Blatz, Deborah Breault, Emily Buell, Nancy L. Buell, Tyler Buell, Joanne Dickinson, Becky Doherty, Suzanne Campo, Mary Crane, Terri Crane, Harold and Mary Dexter, Anne Fenmore, Colbie Fredette, John and Diana Goodhue, Connie Grant, Claudia Jackson, Cindy Keenan, Chris and Brenda Keith, Linda Buell Keith, Linda Knott, JoAnn Fagnant-Langan, Denise McCarthy, Paula McDonald, Sandra McGonagle, Louise McKean, Ellen Mulligan, Sandy Newhall, Maddie Paquette, Laurie Perry, Todd Perry, Pam Seed, Travis and Lindsay and Rachael Shute, Jill Smith, Bette Stafford, Betty Tidd, Abby Thompson, Janelle Vallone, and Becky Wright.

Welch Island Sunset   Photo Courtesy of Nancy Nickerson

LUCKY DAY...
Mark Island ~ Renate Marcoux

My husband Dick came home with some exciting news. "Do we want to buy island property?" he asked. Giving little thought as to how we would pay for it, or how we would get to it, since we had no boat at that time and were unfamiliar with the islands, somehow, amidst the excitement, we decided to take the chance. Sight unseen, we had signed papers by four o'clock that very same afternoon. In retrospect, this was definitely a lucky day for us, a once-in-a-lifetime opportunity without ever having had any regrets.

By early May, we were the proud owners of our first motorized boat, a small Boston Whaler. We packed up the kids, dog, axe, saw, lake chart, and like pioneers, set out on our maiden voyage to claim and set eyes on our little piece of paradise for the very first time. Yet, it was love at first sight! It changed the course of our lifestyle, and because of our enthusiasm, the island fever caught on rapidly. In many cases, we are responsible for having led the way for many of our island neighbors.

After 36 seasons, we still get excited as soon as ice-out is announced. We can embark on another voyage to our beloved island.

Table of Contents

SUMMER FRIENDSHIPS
Lockes Island – Priscilla Mayo Sutcliffe

All islanders know the special bond that exists with their lake neighbors. Without hesitation we lean on each other and find great comfort in just knowing someone who understands is nearby. This camaraderie innocently exists from sharing island experiences on a big lake.

Renewing summer friendships holds a unique sense of excitement and beauty. By nature of limited exposure, we value them differently.

They are, by far, our strongest, most effortless friendships. No doubt, the island atmosphere provides more time to reflect, assess and appreciate life's simpler treasures, where quite naturally these friendships shine brightly.

A PERFECT SUMMER DAY IS WHEN THE SUN IS SHINING, THE BREEZE IS BLOWING, THE BIRDS ARE SINGING, AND THE LAWN MOWER IS BROKEN. James Dent

Full House at the *Witches*

THE LORD HIGH MAYOR OF MINK
Mink Island - Joanne Dickinson

Besides many beautiful high-bush blueberries growing on Mink, we also have huckleberries in abundance, which I first learned about from Bill Veazey. Bill was a wonderful story-teller and font of information regarding island life. We miss him very much now that he has passed on.

Bill's family first settled on Mink years and years ago, along with the Jewett family. Anyway, Bill and his wife Joan sure knew how to make island living fun, and they enjoyed sharing the little peculiarities with newcomers. For example, do you know how to tell the difference between a blueberry and a huckleberry? The blueberries have little crowns, and the huckleberries are smooth and shiny. The deer love both and swim from island to island, grazing on them.

Another long-time resident, Margy Knox, recalls traveling to Mink in the wintertime on a snowmobile years ago, with Bill leading the way. The purpose of Margy's trip was to check on her camp, and the purpose of Bill's trip was to feed the deer – with apples, sacks of horse food, and great big bags of broken potato chips which he finagled from a friend who owned a potato chip factory in Beverly, Massachusetts. Margy said it was quite a sight to see him distributing the food in the snowy woods, with the chickadees fluttering all around him.

We would often visit Bill and Joan to learn what to do, and, more importantly, what not to do, on Mink Island. I always admired the handsomely-carved wooden sign, proclaiming Bill to be the "Lord High Mayor of Mink." I thought I remembered him telling me the story of how friends and well-wishers had presented him with that sign many years before. Just recently his wife Joan corrected me on this point – she remembers him making it for himself!

I know Bill would have loved the show we all enjoyed as Mink Islanders this past summer – watching a baby loon learn to swim and fish, with her parents protectively teaching her the basics. She would often swim right between her parents with her head held proudly, and we all enjoyed seeing her grow from tiny chick to nearly half her parents' size. Most of the residents of Mink had a chance to observe her, as our island is fairly small and the loons can circle it without too much trouble. Several of us were talking about how nice it would have been to see her first flight – another one of the many unique benefits of island life!

We have been on our island for 12 wonderful years. It's our little patch of paradise. Wouldn't trade it for any mega-mansion!

Early Settler...

Straight-Up

Deep Cove Manhattans

Deep Cove Martinis

Flaming Silver Bullets

Mark Island Martini

Lemon Drop Martini

Bellini Martini

Pomegranate Martini

Capt. Goodie's Cosmopolitan

On The Rocks

Mojito

Caipirinha

Frozen

Bushwacker

Slush Sours

Capt. Goodie's Margaritas

For a Crowd

Painkiller

3-Rum Punch

Pink Lemonade Punch

My parents and their friends were all World War II veterans and they loved to have a good party, especially on the 4th of July. The most famous (or infamous) of the lot was the Boat In – Float Out party. Mike Taranto's Chris Craft, the Tana T, was anchored off the shore and arriving guests were flagged down by teenagers in outboards wielding red flags with gold cocktail glasses painted on them. The boaters had a choice between a pitcher of martinis or a pitcher of Manhattans.

Deep Cove Manhattans

Sharon Doyle ❊ Bear Island

To make a pitcher:
1 dash bitters
2 parts whiskey
1 part sweet vermouth

Serve cold, straight up, with cherries.

Deep Cove Martinis

Sharon Doyle ❊ Bear Island

To make a pitcher of very dry martinis:
4 or 5 parts gin
1part dry vermouth

Serve cold, straight up, with olives.

Round Island has been owned by one extended family since the late 1800s, when it was purchased by David Chase Folsom. During the 1970s, it became a tradition for the family to gather in late July to celebrate the birthdays of two island patriarchs, cousins Laurence and Russell Folsom (two of David's three grandsons). These parties often took on a theme: Christmas-in-July, Pirates, Luaus, and even Fantasy Island. In their younger days, the great-great-grandchildren of David (now in their 40s) formed the "Round Island Players" and entertained the adults with skits, comedy routines, music and dancing.

Food was always a big part of all our celebrations on the island, with Great Aunt Rheta Folsom's baked beans, Auntie Barbara Alden's salmon mousse, Grammy Alice Folsom's lemon meringue pie, my mother Anne Marie's (Anne Marie Folsom Ierardi) swinging meatballs and Kahlua trifle and my dad Bob's (Bob Ierardi) flaming silver bullets, which were often served by moonlight at the beach after the kids had been safely tucked in.

Flaming Silver Bullets
Robert Ierardi ❋ Round Island

Cheers from the big house on Round Island!

Pour equal parts of *Drambuie* and Triple Sec into a pony glass. Gently float brandy over top and light carefully.

Note: Lighting the drink is much easier if you fill the pony glass with the first two ingredients and leave only enough room in the glass for the brandy to float on top.

Caution…remember to blow out the flame before drinking!

Round Island Luau and Pirate Parties
Photos courtesy of Robert Ryan

Mark Island Martini

Tom Haughey ✳ Mark Island

When you're on an island, you often need to improvise, and improvising can lead to unexpected results—like substituting radishes as garnish for our martinis when no olives or lemons can be found. It's pretty and tasty.

2~3 ounces of your favorite vodka or gin
1 capful of your favorite dry vermouth
1 medium or 2 small red radishes
Ice

Shake and pour into a stemmed martini glass or serve in a rocks glass over ice.

Lemon Drop Martini

John Goodhue ✳ Mark Island

Remember that this is a real martini, so be careful.

Start with a large shaker half-full of ice.
Add:
6 shots of Citron Vodka (*Absolute* works well)
1 shot of frozen lemonade concentrate
½ shot triple sec
½ shot sour mix

Cover and shake well.

Lemon wedges
Superfine sugar

Chill your martini glasses in the freezer for 30 minutes.
Run a lemon wedge around the rim of the well-chilled martini glass. Dip the rim in a saucer of superfine sugar.
Pour your well-shaken drink and enjoy!

Do you like your drink frozen? If so, make this in a blender, adding lots of ice. Mix for 15 to 25 seconds at high speed. Pour into a martini glass or an 8 ounce old-fashioned glass. Enjoy!

3-Rum Punch

Jeannette Buell ✳ Mark Island

Refreshing and not too sweet, this is a great crowd pleaser.

2 quarts *Ruby Red* grapefruit juice
3 (33.8-ounce) containers *Ceres* mango juice
1 cup unsweetened cranberry juice (*Just Cranberry*)
1 liter sparkling water
1½ cups *Bacardi* light rum
1½ cups *Gosling's Black Seal Rum*
3 cups *Myers's Rum*
1 orange, sliced thin

Mix all ingredients together in a 2-gallon drink cooler with a spigot. Put out a cooler full of ice and a stack of cups so guests can serve themselves.

Note: To keep the punch cold without diluting, float 3 or 4 frozen mini bottles of water (washed, with labels removed) in the punch container.

Pink Lemonade Punch

Daryl Thompson ✳ Welch Island

Adapted From the Cheese Cake Factory

Frozen pink lemonade
Absolute Citron vodka
Chambord raspberry liquor
Lemons for rimming glasses
Flavored sugar for rimming glasses
Fresh or frozen raspberries for garnish

Prepare lemonade; add vodka and *Chambord.* Stir. Pour into glasses filled with ice and rimmed with sugar. Depending on quantity needed, here are suggested proportions:

For one tall glass:
8 ounces lemonade
2 ounces vodka
1 ounce *Chambord*

To one quart of lemonade, add:
1 cup vodka
½ cup *Chambord*

A Breezy Day on Hot Tub

Cold

Marinated Shrimp Cocktail

Green Onion Dip

Olive Salsa

Black Bean Salsa

Texas Hot Salsa

Green Apple Salsa

Tortilla Roll-ups

Layered Mexican Dip

Hot

Swinging Meatballs

Roasted Garlic

Goat Cheese and Chutney Bruschetta

Fig and Blue Cheese Bruschetta

Spinach and Cheese Bread

Black Cat Appetizer

Island Quesadillas

Scooby Snacks

Pepperoni Pizza Dip

Happy Hour Crayfish

Spicy Shrimp

Grilled Peel & Eat Shrimp

Texas Hot Salsa

Stephanie Knighton ❋ Two Mile Island

1 (20-ounce) can whole or diced tomatoes, undrained
1 bunch green onions, chopped
1 bunch cilantro, washed, stems removed
3-6 jalapenos, cut in half, stems, pith and seeds removed
1 tablespoon olive oil
½ teaspoon salt
½ teaspoon ground black pepper
½ teaspoon garlic powder

Put all ingredients into an electric blender and blend well.
Chill about 24 hours, allowing the flavors to develop.

Serve as a dip with tortilla chips or over scrambled eggs.

Green Apple Salsa

Jeannette Buell ❋ Mark Island

This recipe is a signature dish from our friend Linda Knott.
The ingredients make for a colorful, flavorful and refreshing salsa.

2 cups chopped plum tomatoes (about 4)
1 cup chopped Granny Smith apple
½ cup chopped cucumber
½ cup corn kernels
½ cup chopped red pepper
½ cup chopped green onion
¼ cup chopped red onion
2½ tablespoons chopped fresh cilantro
1½ tablespoons fresh lime juice
1 tablespoon chopped, seeded jalapeno pepper
1 tablespoon balsamic vinegar
1½ teaspoons sugar
¾ teaspoon salt
¾ teaspoon pepper

Though labor intensive, this is best when the apple and vegetables are cut to the
same size as the corn kernels. Please do not use a food processor.
Combine all ingredients in a mixing bowl. Toss to coat.
Keep refrigerated until ready to serve.
Serve with tortilla or corn chips.

Tortilla Roll-ups with Salsa

Bobbe Fairman ✳ Camp Island

2 (8-ounce) packages cream cheese, softened
1 (3-ounce) can chopped or sliced black olives
½ small onion, finely chopped
1 package *Good Seasons* Ranch Dressing mix
4-5 large flour tortillas

Blend together cream cheese, black olives, chopped onion, and ranch dressing mix.

Divide and spread cream cheese mixture on tortillas. Roll each tortilla tightly and wrap well in plastic wrap. Chill and slice into ¾ inch pieces.

Serve with salsa.

✳ ✳ ✳ ✳ ✳

B's HIVES
Little Bear Island – Patti Bezanson Fielding

I am second generation on Little Bear Island. Mom and Dad bought the property in 1967, and we four girls have enjoyed life on Little Bear since.

Our families (11 children, ranging from 4 to 30 years old) continue to enjoy island life. Now my grandchildren are enjoying it, too. The five-year-old said to her other grandparents, "The camp is the best place in the whole world!" She's got that right.

We have two cottages, side-by-side, with a third being built. They are called the B's Hive and the B's Hive II, for our last name "Bezanson." Mom and Dad's little haven will be B's Hive III.

One of the greatest things that often takes place is when we all get together and a wonderful meal results, without any planning. Everyone brings something for the grill and a side dish to share. You never know what it's going to be, but it's always amazing. I think the secret is the place-- and the people-- that make it so wonderful.

It's interesting that nothing on the island has really changed for me: more kids, we're older, and more boats on the lake for sure. When I step on the boat and leave the mainland dock, I head back to the same place I remember when I was 10.

Layered Mexican Dip

Jenny Gemberling ❋ Barndoor Island

A casual favorite – our boys and their friends love it!

¼ teaspoon garlic powder
¼ teaspoon chili powder
1 bunch fresh green onions, chopped (divided)
1 (15-ounce) can refried black beans
3 ripe avocadoes, peeled and mashed
1 cup sour cream
½ package taco seasoning
8 ounces Pepper Jack cheese, grated
2 large tomatoes, diced

1 giant bag of corn chips

Mix garlic powder, chili powder and one-third of the chopped green onions into the refried beans. Spread the bean mixture onto your favorite serving platter. Top the beans with mashed avocados. Mix together the sour cream and taco seasoning and spread over avocado layer. Sprinkle the cheese on top. This can be made in advance to this point.
When ready to serve, top with diced tomatoes and the remaining green onions. Serve with corn chips.

Note: Chopped mild green chilies may be substituted for green onions, if desired.

Avocados:

When cooking with avocados, it's best to plan ahead since it is nearly impossible to find a perfectly ripened avocado on the grocer's shelf.

To ripen a rock-hard avocado in one to three days, place it in a paper bag with an apple, banana or tomato. Close the paper bag and let it sit at room temperature. This traps the ethylene gas they produce and helps them to ripen. Never store unripe (hard) avocados in the refrigerator.
To prolong the life of an already ripe avocado, store it in the crisper drawer of your refrigerator. An avocado is ripe when the skin darkens and "gives" slightly when gently squeezed.

Swinging Meatballs

Anne Marie Folsom Ierardi ❋ Round Island

Meatballs:
1 pound ground beef
¼ cup bread crumbs
1 small onion, minced
1 egg
½ cup cooked white rice, cooled
2 teaspoons brown sugar
1 teaspoon lemon juice
Dash garlic powder
Salt and pepper

Combine ground beef, bread crumbs, onion, egg, rice, brown sugar, lemon juice, garlic powder, salt and pepper. Form into cocktail-sized balls.
Brown meatballs in a skillet, in a small amount of oil.

Sauce:
1 cup ketchup
1 cup grape jelly
¼ cup seedless raisins
1 teaspoon lemon juice
1 small onion, diced

Preheat over to 300°F.
Combine sauce ingredients in a small sauce pan.
Heat over medium heat for 10 minutes, stirring well.
Coat meatballs in the warmed sauce and turn into an ovenproof baking dish.
Bake for 25–30 minutes.

Light House at Winter Harbor Yacht Club on Welch Island

Roasted Garlic

Island ❈ Basics

To roast garlic:
Slice the top off a whole bulb of garlic. Drizzle with oil, sprinkle with a little salt and wrap in foil.
Bake at 350°F. for 40-45 minutes or cook on the grill until the cloves are roasted golden brown and are soft like butter. Cool.
Squeeze roasted garlic cloves from the bulb, reserving as much of the now-garlicky oil as you can.

OR you can peel the cloves individually and place them inside a foil pouch with the oil – roast as directed above.

OR you can microwave the garlic cloves for 10 seconds. The skin should slip right off.

Goat Cheese and Chutney Bruschetta

Suzanne Morrissey ❈ Bear Island

We usually keep it super casual on the island, but if someone new is coming to visit, we may make an appetizer that requires more than opening a bag of chips and a jar of salsa.

A head of garlic
Olive oil
A baguette, sliced into half-inch thick rounds
Soft goat cheese
Chutney, any flavor (apple or mango are my favorites)

Roast the garlic, using olive oil (See recipe above.)
Lightly toast the baguette slices and then brush with the garlic oil.
Spread each slice with a small amount of the roasted garlic and goat cheese.
Top with a dollop of chutney.

Fig and Blue Cheese Bruschetta

Bob & Carol Jones ❋ Welch Island

1 French baguette, sliced
3-ounces cream cheese, softened
2-ounces blue cheese, crumbled
½ cup fig preserves or fig jam

Preheat broiler.

Arrange bread slices on a baking sheet.
Broil 1-2 minutes on each side until lightly toasted.

Blend together cream cheese and blue cheese.
Spread the cheese mixture on toasted bread slices.
Top each slice with ½ teaspoon fig preserves.
Return to oven and broil until bubbly.

Spinach and Cheese Bread

Daryl Thompson ❋ Welch Island

A favorite appetizer from the recipe files of our friend, Chip Blaisdell.

2 loaves frozen bread dough
1 (9-ounce) package frozen chopped spinach, thawed and squeezed dry
2 cups grated cheese (Cheddar, Monterey Jack, provolone or mozzarella)
1 cup chopped salami or ham (optional)
1 egg, beaten
1 teaspoon sugar

Thaw bread dough. Roll out the two separate pieces of dough as large as you can, on a lightly-floured surface.

Evenly spread half the spinach and half the cheese over each piece of dough, leaving a little bit of an edge.

Carefully roll up each piece of dough, shaping into a ring, and place on a baking sheet.

Cover with a damp towel and put in a warm, draft-free place. Let rise.
Brush with egg and sprinkle with sugar.
Bake at 350°F. for 1 hour.

Happy Hour Crayfish

Moulton Family ❄ Sleeper Island

The crayfish traps are set in the evening, baited with scraps of the dinner meal.

In the early morning, we check the traps and cook our catch in salt brine with fresh dill – leaving them to marinate until happy hour.

❄ ❄ ❄ ❄ ❄

BIG CAMP ISLAND
Camp Island - Thaddeus and Virginia Thorne

A beautiful place on this earth...

My grandmother, Anna Brown Chandler, was related to the Browns on Long Island. She inherited Little Camp and Big Camp Island from ancestors, along with the first camp on the islands. She gave my father a piece of land on the north end of Big Camp Island in the early 1930s.

My father, Lawton Brown Chandler, and my mother, Esther, and my siblings, Kenneth and Joyce, and I camped in tents while building a small summer camp. For many years (15!) during the 30's and 40's, we never left the island in the summer!

We enjoyed the fresh clean water for drinking, swimming and fishing. Fresh bass, perch, hornpout, crawfish, and large frogs would be caught for frying in the big cast-iron frying pan. The high-bush blueberries next to the beach were great in pies, pancakes and muffins.

In the 1950s through the 80s, Lawton and Esther cooked on a large homemade grill-barbeque chicken, hamburgers, frankfurters, and corn-on-the-cob. Esther's potato salad, coleslaw, baking powder biscuits and fresh strawberries with whipped cream were favorites for their 15 grandchildren! It took 2 or 3 boat trips from Glendale to get everyone to the island.

P.S. My sister Joyce married the boy (Bruce Borden) from the next island – Jolly!

Spicy Shrimp

Renee and Craig Richard ✳ Bear Island

1 pound uncooked shrimp, peeled and deveined

Marinade:
½ cup olive oil
2 tablespoons lemon juice
1 tablespoon honey
1 tablespoon soy sauce
2 tablespoons chopped fresh parsley
2 tablespoons Cajun or Creole seasoning
Pinch of cayenne pepper

French bread

Blend together marinade ingredients and add shrimp.
Turn into a 12x8-inch baking dish.
Cover and refrigerate for 1 hour before cooking.

Preheat oven to 450°F.
Bake for 10 minutes or until shrimp are cooked.
Serve with French bread, to dip in the flavored oil.

Grilled Peel-and-Eat Shrimp

Anne A. Hummel ✳ Mark Island

2 pounds unpeeled, extra-large shrimp
Extra-virgin olive oil
Sea salt
Pepper
Your favorite seasoning: *Old Bay*, chili powder or Asian spices

Place the shrimp in a bowl with a good drizzle of olive oil, salt, pepper and seasoning. Toss to coat.
Preheat the grill to high heat. Oil the grates with non stick spray or olive oil.
Place the marinated shrimp on the grill. Cook, turning once - they cook quickly.
Remove from the grill to a platter.
Serve with plenty of napkins and a bowl for the peels.
Don't forget to enjoy the view…

TRACTOR PULL
Treasure Island– Claudette Gammon

It all started one fine summer evening during the annual Treasure Island Cocktail Party. One of our neighbors, Ken Meyers, had just received a brand new tractor from his wife Debbie for his birthday. It was a Craftsman, a fine-looking piece of machinery!

After a few drinks, it was decided to pit that Craftsman tractor against a tried and true old friend, a 35-year-old International Harvester owned by West Frazier, and an Ariens lawn mower owned by Rodney Gammon.

The lawn mower was allowed to participate because it was a riding mower. How could it possibly win against the Craftsman? Plus it was the only other item on the island that was CLOSE to being a tractor. And what could be easier than to beat the two old souls of Treasure Island?

The next morning we all gathered at the Meyers' compound to start the festivities. It was absolutely amazing what a group of determined people came up with in less than 24 hours.

We found all sorts of objects for this tractor pull and relay race - orange traffic cones and all. A trophy to be awarded to the winner was put together quite cleverly by Doug Burns from a piece of two-by-four, plastic toy shovels, and a toy truck. When it arrived on the field of battle, the paint was still wet!

We had timed races and a race through the middle of the island, where the drivers had to pick up stuff. And then, last but not least, was the tractor pull. Each against the other, the winner of the first pull had to pull against the last one standing, which was the lawn mower.

After all the races were said and done and the pull was finished, Ken Meyers' Craftsman came in dead last. So there is a lot to be said for the old tried and true.

Tractor Race   Photo Courtesy of Claudette Gammon

Mary and Harold Dexter on Dinner Rock, Welch Island

Yeast Breads

Anadama Bread

Fannie Farmer White Bread

Cuban Bread

Welch Island Oatmeal Bread

Soft Pretzels

Cinnamon Rolls

Quick Breads

Shortcut Sticky Buns

Oatmeal Muffins

Morning Glory Muffins

Blueberry Muffins

Low-Fat Blueberry Muffins

Blueberry Buckle

Whortleberry Buckle

Cranberry Scones

Sour Cream Scones

Auntie's Scones

Sweet Flavored Butters

Bear Island Blueberry Scones

Corn Bread

Blueberry Corn Skillet Bread

Boston Brown Bread

Pancakes

Rattlesnake Island

Fast-Acting Blueberry

Loon Island Blueberry

Cheap Syrup

Blueberry Buttermilk

Dutch Baby Pancake

Emergency Breakfast

French Toast

Grand Marnier French Toast

French Toast Strata

Oven French Toast w/Pecans

Eggs

Eggs Benedict

Poached Eggs

Hard-Cooked Eggs

Quiche Lorraine

Crust-less Quiche

Basic Frittata

Cheese Strata

Mark Island

Camp Omelettes

Anadama Bread

Sharon Doyle ✳ Bear Island

Anadama Bread dates back to colonial times. Some say it's an old Indian name. Some say that a colonial newlywed got tired of eating cornmeal mush every night, which was all that his wife, whose name was Anna, could cook. So one night he came home, mixed the mush with flour and yeast, baked it up, served it and said, "Anna, dammit, this is what I want!"

½ cup cornmeal
1 cup lukewarm water, divided
1 package yeast
1½ cups boiling water
3 tablespoons butter
½ cup molasses
2 teaspoons salt
3 cups whole wheat flour
2½ – 3½ cups unbleached white flour
Cornmeal

In a small bowl, mix cornmeal with ¾ cup of water.
In a separate, small bowl, dissolve yeast in remaining warm water. Set aside.

Add mixed cornmeal to boiling water and stir over low heat until mush begins to boil. Remove from heat; add butter, molasses and salt. Let cool. When mush is lukewarm, stir in yeast; transfer to bread bowl.

Stir in whole-wheat flour and enough white flour to make a firm, non-sticky dough. On a lightly floured surface, knead dough for nine minutes. Place dough in a bowl wiped with vegetable oil. Turn dough over, then cover with damp towel. Let rise until double in bulk. Punch down. Knead lightly and then shape into loaves, French loaves, rounds or braids- as you like.

Place on lightly-greased cookie sheets, dusted with cornmeal. Let rise until doubled in bulk.

Bake at 400°F. for 15 minutes, then reduce heat to 375°F.
Bake about 35 minutes longer (less for French breads or braids).

Makes two loaves.

I associate going to the lake with homemade bread. When we first moved into our house on the point of Deep Cove in 1952, there was a large cast-iron stove which my mom, Kay Sauerbrunn, cooked on, and the tradition of homemade bread was established.

Mom would bake this great white bread from her ancient Fannie Farmer cookbook and serve it warm from the oven with butter and raspberry jam. It was the first bread I learned to bake.

My grandmother, Kathleen Handley, who was born in England, served tea on the front porch every afternoon at four. And, of course, tea had to be accompanied by either cinnamon toast or homemade scones. I remember baking these. The fun part for kids was scoring them and then sprinkling them with sugar. There were always bits of dough that didn't make it to the pan.

For the past ten years, my own family, the Doyles, have eaten homemade bread and nothing else while at the lake. My son Nick learned to make pizza dough one summer, and we learned not to play soccer with it, unless we wanted it to taste like cardboard.

Our other favorites are Anadama Bread, which is my oldest son Andrew's favorite, and Cuban Bread, which can be used for everything from really cool French bread to hamburger buns. My daughter, Felicity, learned to make this bread the summer of 2007.

✳ ✳ ✳ ✳ ✳

EVERYBODY NEEDS BEAUTY AS WELL AS BREAD, PLACES TO PLAY IN AND PRAY IN, WHERE NATURE MAY HEAL AND GIVE STRENGTH TO BODY AND SOUL. John Muir

Fannie Farmer White Bread

Sharon Doyle ✳ Bear Island

½ cup lukewarm water
1 package yeast

1 cup boiling water
2 tablespoons butter or shortening
2 tablespoons sugar or honey
1 tablespoon salt
1 cup milk
6-plus cups of all-purpose flour

Dissolve yeast in lukewarm water. Let stand for five minutes.

Combine boiling water, butter, sugar and salt in a large mixing bowl. Stir until butter is melted and sugar is dissolved. Add milk. Cool to lukewarm, and then add yeast to mixture.

Using a wooden spoon, stir in 3 cups of flour and mix thoroughly. Add another 3 cups of flour and stir vigorously.

Add additional flour until the dough no longer sticks to the bowl.

Turn dough out onto floured surface. Cover and let rest for ten minutes.
Knead dough for nine minutes until it is smooth and elastic.

Place dough in a lightly-greased bowl and cover with a damp cloth. Let rise in warm place until doubled in size.

Once dough has risen, punch down and turn out onto a floured surface. Knead lightly and divide in two. Shape into round shepherd's loaves or traditional loaves.

Place on a greased baking sheet or into greased loaf pans, seam side down. Let rise another hour or until double in bulk.

Note: If you don't have a cozy place, dough will rise in cold oven over a pan of hot water.

Bake at 400°F. for 40-50 minutes, until crust is nicely browned and the loaf sounds hollow when thumped with a finger.

Remove bread from pans immediately. Allow loaves to cool on their sides.

Cuban Bread

Sharon Doyle ❋ Bear Island

Quick and easy – a great addition to a spaghetti dinner or made in to hamburger rolls. Take note that this bread is started in a <u>cold</u> oven when baked.

1 package yeast
2 cups lukewarm water
1 ¼ teaspoons salt
1 tablespoon sugar
6-9 cups of unbleached white flour

Dissolve the yeast in water in a large bowl. Add salt and sugar, mixing gently but thoroughly.

Using a wooden spoon, stir in flour, one cup at a time, until you have achieved a smooth dough. Cover with a damp cloth and let rise in a warm spot. *For finer texture*, knead dough lightly on floured surface, then return it to the bowl for its first rise.

Once dough has doubled in size, punch down and turn out onto lightly floured work surface. Knead lightly and shape into French loaves, smaller rolls or Italian rounds. Place on baking sheet, sprinkled with corn meal.
Let rise five minutes.

Brush loaves with cold water. Put loaves in a <u>cold</u> oven. Turn oven on to 400°F. Place a pan of boiling water on the lower rack.

Let bake for 25-45 minutes (depending on the size of your loaves) or until bread is crusty, browned, and has a slightly hollow sound when thumped.

Bear Island Mail Dock

Welch Island Oatmeal Bread

Susan MacBride ✳ Welch Island

1 cup water
1 cup milk
2 tablespoons butter
¼ cup canola or peanut oil

1 cup rolled oats

1½ tablespoons yeast
⅔ cup warm water
2 teaspoons salt
¼ cup sugar
½ cup molasses
5½ – 6 cups flour

Combine milk, water, butter and oil in a sauce pan. Bring to a boil.
Remove from heat. Add oats and stir. Cool to lukewarm.

Dissolve yeast in warm water.

Pour cooled oatmeal mixture into a large mixing bowl.
Add salt, sugar, molasses and yeast mixture.
Beat for 2 minutes with an electric mixer.

Gradually add flour, stirring by hand, until dough no longer sticks to bowl.

Turn dough out onto a floured surface and knead for 8-10 minutes (or use a mixer fitted with a dough hook). Shape dough into a ball and place in a greased bowl.

Cover and let rise until doubled in size.

Preheat oven to 375°F.
Punch down dough and divide in half. Shape and place in 2 greased bread pans. Let rise, covered, until doubled.

Bake for 35-40 minutes.
Remove from pans. Cool loaves on their sides on a wire rack.

Soft Pretzels

Katherine Aceto ❋ Welch Island

This is a great rainy day project with the kids.

2 cups warm water
2 tablespoons dry yeast
½ cup sugar
2 teaspoons salt
2 tablespoons butter, softened
1 egg
6 ½ to 7 ½ cups flour
1 egg yolk
2 tablespoons water
Coarse salt or kosher salt

Pour warm water into a large mixing bowl. Sprinkle in yeast and stir to dissolve. Add sugar, salt, butter, egg, and 3 cups flour.

Beat on medium speed (or by hand) until smooth. Using a large spoon, mix in more flour, one cup at a time. Keep mixing by hand until you have a stiff dough.

Cover bowl with plastic wrap and refrigerate for at least 2 hours, or up to 24 hours.

Turn dough onto floured board. Divide in half; cut each half into 16 pieces. Roll each piece between your hands, into a thin strip about 20 inches long.

Here's the fun part:
Twist and shape into a pretzel shape, your initials, a boat… whatever!
Arrange your pretzels on a lightly greased baking sheet.

Combine the egg yolk with 2 tablespoons of water, mixing with a fork. Brush each pretzel with this mixture.

Sprinkle pretzels lightly with coarse salt, cover them with a clean dish towel and put them in a warm, draft-free place. Let rise about 30 minutes, or until doubled in size.

Preheat oven to 400°F. Bake 15 minutes or until pretzels are lightly browned. Makes about 32.

Note: Try cinnamon-sugar pretzels or pretzel dogs…

Keep~Your~Summer~Job Cinnamon Rolls

Marnie Wells White ✳ Mark Island

My brother and I worked at Shep Brown's Boat Basin every summer. On those weekend mornings, when I started late, I dropped Jamie off at work and sped back to the island to bake cinnamon rolls for all the guys. I kept the job for as long as I wanted it.

Dough:
1 package active dry yeast
¼ cup warm water
1 cup milk, scalded
¼ cup sugar
¼ cup shortening
1 teaspoon salt
3½ cups flour
1 egg

Filling:
4 tablespoons butter, melted
½ cup sugar
2 teaspoons ground cinnamon

Icing:
2 cups powdered sugar
Enough milk or light cream to achieve desired consistency
1 teaspoon vanilla
Dash of salt

Soften yeast in warm water. Set aside. Combine freshly scalded milk, sugar, shortening, and salt in a mixing bowl. Cool to lukewarm.
Add 1½ cups flour, beating well. Beat in yeast and egg.
Add remaining flour to form soft dough, beating well.
Place in a greased bowl, turning once to grease surface.
Let rise until double~1½ to 2 hours.
Turn out onto lightly floured surface and divide the dough in half.

Mix together melted butter, sugar and cinnamon.
Roll each half of dough into a 16x8-inch rectangle.
Spread cinnamon-sugar mixture over each.
Roll up along the long side and seal the edges.
Using unflavored dental floss, cut rolls into 1-inch thick slices.
Place cut-side down onto 1 greased jelly roll pan.
Let rise until doubled, about 30 to 40 minutes.

Bake at 375°F. for 20-25 minutes.
Stir together icing ingredients and spread on hot rolls.
Serve while warm to12 enthusiastic mechanics and dock crew!

Shortcut Sticky Buns

Kathleen Aceto ✳ Welch Island

After an early morning swim, these are a favorite breakfast treat, served with coffee and fruit on the dock.

¾ cup brown sugar
½ cup dark corn syrup
2 teaspoons melted butter
1 can *Pillsbury Grande Biscuits* (in refrigerated section)
1 cup raisins
1 cup walnuts, chopped
Cinnamon

Preheat oven to 350°F. Grease a Bundt pan.
Mix together brown sugar, syrup and butter.
Cut each biscuit into 4 pieces.
Layer ½ the sugar/syrup mixture on bottom of Bundt pan.
Sprinkle with half the raisins and walnuts.
Place 16 pieces of the biscuits evenly on top of raisins.
Sprinkle heavily with cinnamon.
Repeat above process. Bake for about 25 minutes until buns sound hollow when tapped. Immediately invert onto a dish.

✳ ✳ ✳ ✳ ✳

NO DONUTS FOR BREAKFAST
Mark Island - Nancy L. Buell

Irving, myself and our four children, Linda, Debbie, Deems and Bill, spent lots of memorable times camping on Mark Island.

Many a time our dear friends Nancy and Harry Bryant would join us with their three daughters, Ann, Ellen and Susan. During the night on one of our great weekends, we were visited by raccoons with a sweet tooth. The children woke the next morning to find that their favorite breakfast of LaFlamme's jelly donuts had been eaten by the scavengers – all 2 dozen donuts!

Low-Fat Blueberry Muffins

Anne B. Minkoff ❈ Cow Island

Best if baked in an old-type cast-iron muffin tin with longer and narrower muffins, than in tins with round muffins. Makes about 18.

2 cups of pre-sifted flour
½ teaspoon salt
1 tablespoon baking powder
⅓ cup sugar
2 cups blueberries
2 egg whites, slightly beaten
¾ cup skim milk
¼ cup vegetable oil

Preheat oven to 425°F. Oil or spray muffin tins.
Sift together flour, salt, baking powder and sugar.
Add berries to dry ingredients. Mix gently.
In a separate mixing bowl, blend together egg whites, milk and oil. Add wet ingredients to dry ingredients. Stir quickly and lightly. If more moisture is needed, add a little more milk.
Spoon batter into tins, filling to ⅔ full.
Bake 25 minutes, or until lightly browned.
Remove from oven and pierce each muffin with a small knife to let steam out.
Tip muffins in tin to vent.
Wait 5-10 minutes before removing from baking tins.

Note: Some advance prep can be done the night before.
Mix separately the dry and wet ingredients. Cover and keep dry ingredients at room temperature, but refrigerate wet ingredients. In the morning, continue with mixing and baking instructions.

GROWING UP ON THE BARBER POLE
Cow Island - Anne B. Minkoff

My family has enjoyed summer living on Winnipesaukee since my grandfather built the first family "camp" on the Barber's Pole in 1905. In 1973 my husband and I moved to nearby Cow Island. My sister, cousins and our families recently celebrated our 100th anniversary on the lake.

One of my favorite things about Lake Winnipesaukee is the blueberries. I have modified my grandmother's recipe for blueberry muffins. They are something I really look forward to in the summer.

Blueberry Buckle

Maria Found ❄ Melody Island

Melody Island has wild blueberry bushes from which we often pick while traveling the 'blueberry trail' on the island. They are plentiful and there is nothing better than waking up to a breakfast of blueberry waffles, blueberry pancakes, or blueberry buckle!

2~2 ½ cups fresh or partially frozen blueberries
2 cups of sifted, all-purpose flour
2 teaspoons baking powder
½ teaspoon salt
5 tablespoons unsalted butter, softened
¾ cup sugar
1 large egg
½ cup milk

Topping:
½ cup sugar
⅓ cup sifted, all-purpose flour
1 teaspoon cinnamon
3 tablespoons unsalted butter, softened

Preheat oven to 375°F. Lightly butter an 8 or 9-inch square baking pan.
Toss blueberries with a small amount of the measured flour.
Sift together remaining flour, baking powder and salt. Set aside.

In a large mixing bowl, cream butter and sugar for about 3 minutes.
Add the egg and continue beating until light and fluffy.
Add in the dry ingredients, alternating with the milk in 3 to 4 additions.
Gently fold in the blueberries.
Pour batter into the prepared pan. Set aside.

Topping: Combine sugar, flour and cinnamon in a small bowl. Cut in the butter with a fork to make a crumbly mixture. Sprinkle over cake batter.

Bake 30-35 minutes or until a toothpick comes out clean. Serve warm or cold. Top with whipped cream or ice cream.

Whortleberry Buckle

Gail Pillow ❋ Whortleberry Island

This recipe is a summer favorite at our camp.
The buckle is packed with our favorite summer fruit.

¼ cup butter
¾ cup sugar
1 egg
1 teaspoon vanilla
2 cups sifted flour
2 teaspoons baking powder
¼ teaspoon salt
½ teaspoon cinnamon
⅛ teaspoon nutmeg
½ cup milk
3 cups blueberries + 1 cup blueberries

Topping:
⅔ cup sugar
⅓ cup flour
½ teaspoon cinnamon
¼ teaspoon nutmeg
¼ cup butter

Preheat oven to 350°F. Grease an 11x7x1½-inch pan.

Cream together butter and sugar. Beat in egg and vanilla.
Sift together flour, baking powder, salt, cinnamon and nutmeg.
Add alternately to creamed mixture with milk.

Gently mix in 3 cups of the blueberries.

Spread mixture in pan. Top with remaining cup of blueberries.
Mix topping ingredients together by hand to create a coarse crumble.
Sprinkle crumble over the top of the buckle.
Bake for approximately 45-60 minutes.
Serves 10

❋ ❋ ❋ ❋ ❋

Whortleberries are European blueberries, having pink flowers and blue or blackish
edible berries, with a powdery bloom...also known as huckleberries or hurtleberries.

Cranberry Scones

Jennifer Mason Malafey ❈ Welch Island

2 cups flour
1 tablespoon baking powder
¾ teaspoon salt
⅓ cup sugar, plus more to sprinkle on top
1 cup dried cranberries
1¼ cup heavy cream
2 tablespoons melted butter

Sift together flour, baking powder, salt and sugar in a bowl.
Stir in dried cranberries.
Drizzle in heavy cream, mixing with a fork until sticky.
Turn out onto a floured surface and knead 10 times.
Form in to a circle and cut in to 10 triangles.
Arrange on a baking sheet. Brush tops with melted butter and sprinkle with additional sugar.
Bake at 425°F. for 15-17 minutes.

Sour Cream Scones

Kathleen Aceto ❈ Welch Island

2 cups flour
½ cup sugar
½ teaspoon baking soda
½ teaspoon salt
½ cup butter, softened
1 egg, beaten
½ cup sour cream
Optional: cinnamon chips, dried cranberries, blueberries…

Preheat oven to 375°F.
Blend flour, sugar, soda and salt. Cut in butter until mealy.
Add the egg to the sour cream and fold into dry ingredients.
Place dough on floured surface and shape in to a circle about ¼ – ½ inch thick.
Cut in to circles or triangles.
Place on a baking sheet and bake for 15 to 20 minutes.

Rattlesnake Island Pancakes

Jeannie Leach ✳ Rattlesnake Island

1½ cups flour
3 tablespoons sugar
1 teaspoon salt
1¾ teaspoons baking powder
2 eggs
1 cup milk
3 tablespoon butter, melted
Extra butter for frying

Mix together dry ingredients: flour, sugar, salt and baking powder.

Lightly beat the eggs in a separate bowl, then add milk and butter. Blend.
Add dry ingredients to the wet, mixing only enough to moisten.

Cook pancakes in butter, pouring the batter from a pitcher into the center of the pancake. This creates better shaped circles.

Flip the pancakes when the centers bubble and the edges brown.

✳ ✳ ✳ ✳ ✳

Emily Buell Picking Blueberries
Photo courtesy of Jill Buell

Fast-Acting Blueberry Pancakes

Jim Wells ✳ Mark Island

4 cups pancake or waffle mix (not the "complete" kind)
4 eggs
8 tablespoons melted butter
1 (14-ounce) can evaporated milk
14 ounces water
2 cups wild blueberries, fresh, frozen or canned.

If you like purple pancakes, add juice from the canned variety as a substitute for some of the above liquid.

For larger crowds, one egg can be added for each additional cup of dry mix.

Mix all ingredients, adding the blueberries last.
Note: The secret of *fast-acting* is a small (3-4 inch) thin pancake.
Cook in a pan or on a griddle. Flip when bubbles appear.
If large, high-bush blueberries are used, the thin pancakes will stand off the surface and not cook properly, so "whap" each with a spatula after turning to flatten the berries.

If you discover any cooked pancakes that happen to have no blueberries, they may, with good wrist action and a "whoops," be flipped high in the general direction of the table.

> *Scoring as follows:*
> *0 points for landing on ground or floor*
> *1 point for landing on the table*
> *3 points for landing on someone's plate*
> *5 points for landing in a cup of coffee*

Before the meal is finished, make sure the outhouse door is unlocked.

THE RESTORATION OF NIPPLE ROCK
Mark Island - Ray Keating and Jim Wells

Light #46 lies on the northeast end of Round Island. It is one of the few navigation marks in the area that is embedded in a large bolder. This mark is called Nipple Rock. Mother Nature works on Nipple Rock to break away facets of its rock-face over time. As a result, various island factions have, with some loosely defined sense of responsibility, taken it upon themselves to repair the ravages of nature. Some years ago the following call-to-action was presented to the residents of Mark Island:

Nearly Invisible Protuberance Provides Little Enthusiasm
Rebuild Our Crumbling Knip

Sailors of the Mark Island Navy, you are once again called into service for the good of all mankind (or at least boaters on the lake). The once proud erection known as Nipple Rock has crumbled into a sagging, stretch-marked shadow of its former self. No longer able to nurture disoriented sailors, it must be brought back to its former fullness or suffer a radical mastectomy at the hands of the dreaded Safety Patrol, more recently made famous for arresting topless boaters within a "No Wake" area near what was once called Jolly Island.

This very Sunday, under cover of first light, all crewmen are called to attend the initial stages of cosmetic surgery to restore that proud beacon to its former firmness. Once the aging tissue (mortar) has been replaced, and a suitable healing period elapses, (a week or so), the color, a familiar red, will be brushed lightly on all surfaces to stimulate our beauty in to full bloom – once again to feel the gentle caress of morning fog and passing seagull.

Under the skilled-hand of Captain, and chief mason, 'Poo Bah' Wells, you will be instructed in the finer arts of nipple repair. The MV 'Barge' will be on station with ample supplies to see you through the challenging task, so lay to and give a hand, boys!

Under a low-lying fog the intrepid crew set forth to perform its re-constructive surgery. Given the early hours, it is uncertain how much beer was consumed, but the project went swimmingly, and the re-construction was viewed as a great success. The crew and the ladies auxiliary retired to the Wells' outdoor cookery for the Wells' famous *Fast-Acting Blueberry Pancakes.*

ISLAND BLUEBERRY PANCAKES
Mark Island – Tom and Marcia Haughey

It's all about the blueberries. The shores of the islands are covered with berry bushes. Most are low-bush, a.k.a. huckleberry bushes, but here and there are naturally growing high-bush blueberry bushes which produce tiny sweet-tart, fabulous blueberries from about the 4th week in July to the end of August.

It's not always easy to tell the bushes apart, since some low-bush grow quite tall and some high-bush do not. Tom once sent a guest out to gather some blueberries. The guest soon proudly returned with a mug brimming with berries. Tom took a careful look at the berries and immediately tossed them into the bushes. The guest was horrified. Tom then gave the guest some tips on distinguishing huckleberries from blueberries and sent him back out among the bushes.

One way to distinguish between the two is to sample the berries. The huckleberries have seeds and are not sweet. The blueberries have no seeds and are sweet, and what makes them special, they are also tart...totally unlike the giant just-sweet store bought variety.

If you kayak or canoe the shores of the islands, you'll be able to see the trunks/branches of the bushes fairly easily and, thereby, distinguish the high-bush from the low. When hiking, however, we've found that the best way to tell them apart is to take a close look at the berries themselves. The blueberries have tiny crowns opposite the stems, and the huckleberries do not.

The rest is easy. Get a box of Bisquick, a jug of NH maple syrup, a quart of milk, an egg and some butter and follow the directions on the box, sprinkling a small handful of the blueberries onto each pancake just before you flip them.

Loon Island Blueberry Pancakes

Tower Family ❋ Loon Island

Ed, Julie, Kate and Betsy have submitted this recipe in loving memory of their mother, Eleanor Winslow Crane Tower Schlosberg, who received Loon Island as a Christmas present in the early 1930's, when countless island blueberry traditions began.

Loon Island blueberries are particularly succulent because of the 360-degree exposure to Winnipesaukee breezes and full-day sun.

First thing in the morning, pick 2 or more cups of island blueberries – depending on the size of the mob. *(For picking, wear a vintage, stretched-out, one-size-fits-all bathing suit spattered with a litany of house paint and roofing gook in order to avoid stains on PJs.)*

Sort the blueberries, taking particular care to remove pine needles, tiny spiders, and cottony spider webs.

1 cup milk
2 tablespoons butter, melted
1 egg, beaten
1 cup flour
2 teaspoons baking powder
2 teaspoons sugar
Pinch of salt

Make the batter by blending together, first the wet, then the dry ingredients. Stir until just moistened.

Preheat a cast-iron griddle on the stove, straddling the burners.

Oil the griddle and cook nice, thin, crispy pancakes with as many blueberries sprinkled on top of the wet batter as possible.

Serve with "Cheap Syrup" (recipe follows) or New Hampshire maple syrup to bed-headed guests as they appear from the outlying bunkhouse, annex or cabin.

Enjoy the view and the pancakes with your beloved friends, family, first-timers, and return island-worshippers, surrounded by choppy or smooth waters, brilliant sunshine or invigorating mist, towering pines and the anticipation of another memorable day on the island.

Cheap Syrup

Recipe as outlined on the bottle of Mapleline

1 cup boiling water
2 cups sugar
½ teaspoon *Mapleline* (imitation maple flavor)

Bring water and sugar to a boil in a saucepan.
Boil for 5 minutes. Remove from heat. Stir in flavoring.
Serve warm or at room temperature.

Blueberry Buttermilk Pancakes

Margy Knox ❋ Mink Island

The islands are full of high-bush blueberries, which become ripe in mid to late July. In 2007 they were larger and sweeter than I ever remember, probably due to the unusually high water and rain in June. I first learned to love wild blueberries from my aunt Parkie Fisher who had a small cabin on the north side of Mink Island and a very large group of blueberry bushes from which she made many wonderful coffee cakes, muffins and blueberry pie. My favorite recipe using wild blueberries is Blueberry Buttermilk Pancakes…

2 eggs, separated
2 cups buttermilk
1 cup flour
1 pinch salt
1 teaspoon baking soda, dissolved in 1-2 teaspoons water
2 tablespoons melted butter
¼ cup wild island blueberries (or more as you like)

Mix together the egg yolks, buttermilk, flour, salt and baking soda. Set aside. Beat egg whites until foamy but not dry. Fold into the batter just before cooking. Stir in melted butter and blueberries.

Wipe a hot griddle with a pat of butter, blotting any excess with a paper towel. Spoon batter onto griddle. Cook until holes appear (until pancake looks something like a sponge), then flip and cook a few minutes more. Transfer the cooked pancakes to a warming plate and continue until all are cooked.

Makes approximately 12 medium pancakes.

Serve with real New Hampshire-made maple syrup.

❋ ❋ ❋ ❋ ❋

Note: To substitute 1 cup of buttermilk, stir together 1 cup of milk and 2 teaspoons lemon juice.

Eggs Benedict

Harold Dexter ❄ Welch Island

Doc Dexter's signature Sunday-morning specialty!

2 English muffins, split, toasted
4 slices Canadian bacon or ham, warmed
4 poached eggs
½ cup Hollandaise sauce

To assemble:
Place 2 toasted English muffin halves on each plate. Top muffins with warmed bacon or ham; place a poached egg on top of each muffin and drizzle 2 tablespoons of Hollandaise sauce on each poached egg.

Poached Eggs

Island ❄ Basics

Spray a medium-size saucepan with cooking spray; fill halfway with water.
Bring water to a simmer over medium heat - don't let water boil.
Crack eggs one at a time into a small cup and slide into the simmering water.
Simmer 3-5 minutes, until the whites are cooked and the yolk is still soft.
With a slotted spoon, transfer the eggs onto a plate.

Note: Eggs can be pre-cooked and kept on a plate at this point. Reheat by sliding egg into simmering water for 1 minute.

Hard-Cooked Eggs

Island ❄ Basics

Place eggs in a pan of cold water and bring to a rolling boil.
Cover pan and turn off heat. Let sit for 20 minutes.
Drain eggs; crack and roll to remove shells.

Quiche Lorraine

Daryl Thompson ✳ Welch Island

1 (10-inch) pie crust
12 strips of bacon, crisply cooked and crumbled
1 cup grated Swiss cheese
4 eggs, slightly beaten
2 cups light cream or milk
Salt
Pepper
Paprika

Preheat oven to 450°F.
Line a deep-dish pie plate with crust.
Sprinkle bacon and Swiss cheese into the bottom of lined pie plate.
Beat eggs slightly; blend in cream.
Pour egg mixture over bacon and cheese; season with salt, pepper, paprika.
Bake at 450°F. for 15 minutes, then lower heat to 350°F.
Continue to cook for another 30 minutes.

Crust-less Quiche

Jeannette Buell ✳ Mark Island

If you are living low-carb or have a wheat allergy, this will appeal to you.

Preheat the oven according to your recipe.

You will need a roasting pan large enough to accommodate the pie plate or baking dish. Lay a dish towel or several layers of paper towels in the bottom of the pan. This has now become your water bath or *ban-marie*.

Place your *bain-marie* on the middle rack of a preheated oven. Carefully transfer your filled baking dish to the center of the pan. Fill the *bain-marie* with enough scalding-hot tap water to come half-way up the sides of the baking dish.

Carefully slide the rack back into the oven, close the door.
Bake according to your recipe.

Frittata

The frittata is an Italian dish, similar to an omelette. Unlike an omelette, the egg mixture is not folded over. Most variations of the frittata start with a few moments on the stove-top until the filling ingredients are heated through and the bottom layer of the egg mixture has solidified. The frittata is then finished in the oven or under the broiler. Making a frittata is a great way to use up leftovers.

Basic Frittata

Louise McKean ❋ Mark Island

6 large eggs
2 tablespoons heavy cream
½ teaspoon salt
½ teaspoon ground pepper
Butter or oil for sautéing the filling

Filling suggestions:
Vegetables, fresh or cooked, then chopped
Meat or seafood, cooked and chopped
Cheese, grated or cubed

In a mixing bowl, whisk together the eggs, cream, salt and pepper.

Once you have chosen your fillings, cook or reheat the vegetables and meat in an ovenproof non-stick skillet, coated with butter or oil.

Pour the egg mixture over the hot vegetables and meat.
Sprinkle the cheese on top. Cover and cook over medium heat until the frittata is almost set, 2-3 minutes.

Uncover and place under the broiler to finish setting the top.

The frittata should be golden brown and have the texture of a very stiff omelette. Slice into wedges and serve immediately.

❋ ❋ ❋ ❋ ❋

Note: If you want to increase this recipe, the rule of thumb is 1 egg per person with the addition of 1 teaspoon of cream per egg.

Strata

Strata is a terrific way to make an egg dish that can be prepared in advance, except for the baking. It's perfect for a holiday morning when you want something a little special, or when you have guests sleeping over. Here's a recipe for a basic cheese strata. From here, embellish with the addition of your favorite ingredients or with what you have on hand.

Cheese Strata

Daryl Thompson ❋ Welch Island

2 cups (3 slices) bread cubes, crusts trimmed
8-ounces sharp Cheddar cheese, cubed
½ pound bacon, cooked and crumbled
4 tablespoons butter, melted
8-ounces whole fresh mushrooms
3 large eggs
2 cups milk
1 teaspoon prepared mustard
¼ teaspoon salt

Butter a 1½ quart baking dish.
Place half the bread cubes in the prepared dish. Layer with half the cheese, bacon and butter. Repeat layers and arrange mushrooms on top.
Beat together eggs, milk, mustard and salt.
Pour over layered mixture.
Cover and refrigerate overnight, if possible.

Preheat oven to 300°F.
Set the baking dish in a pan of hot water on the center rack in the oven.
Bake uncovered for 1½ hours.

Note: Ham, sausage or shrimp may be substituted for bacon.

Other flavor options:
Onion bagels, Havarti with dill and smoked salmon
Corn muffins, Pepper Jack and mild green chilies
French bread, herbed or plain Brie and seeded, chopped tomatoes

Mark Island Camp Omelettes

Mary Anne and Kim Baron ✳ Mark Island

8 eggs, separated
Salt and pepper to taste
2 tablespoons crème fraiche
Butter
Herbs: parsley, chervil and tarragon

Separate the egg yolks from the whites into 2 separate bowls.
Beat the yolks with salt and fresh ground pepper.
Whisk the whites, not so much as to make them stiff.

Lightly whip the crème fraiche in its own bowl.
Put a knob of butter in the omelette pan over high heat.
Once the butter starts to sizzle, add the yolks.
Wait until the yolks are nearly set, and then cover with the crème fraiche.
Pour the egg whites on top.
The omelette should be cooked over high heat for no more than 3 minutes. Fold the omelette over and slide it onto a serving dish.
Sprinkle with melted butter and herbs.

Serves 4

Note: Crème Fraiche is a soured, cultured-cream product, originally from France, similar to sour cream. The smooth, thick cream is tangy and sweet, with a slightly nutty flavor. It can be found in the cheese section of your local grocery store.

Homemade Crème Fraiche

Mary Anne and Kim Baron ✳ Mark Island

To make 1 cup of crème fraiche, combine 1 cup heavy cream and 1 tablespoon buttermilk in a small saucepan over medium-low heat. Heat to lukewarm--do not allow it to simmer.

Remove from the heat, cover, and allow it to thicken at warm room temperature. This can take from 8 hours to 48 hours, depending on your taste and recipe needs.

Once it is as thick and flavorful as you want it, refrigerate it to chill well before using.

An Outhouse of the Finest Kind

Soups

    Italian Wedding Soup

    White Gazpacho

    Hamburger Soup

    Turkey Vegetable Soup

    Caribbean Coconut Soup

Chilis

    Vegetarian Chili

    White Turkey Chili

    Garnasiska Chili

Stews

    Bean Pot Stew

    Hot Diggity Stew

Chowder

    Clam Chowder for Fifty Trekers

Bisque

    Lobster Bisque

Italian Wedding Soup

Walter Johnson ❄ Little Bear Island

1 tablespoon olive oil
1 clove garlic, chopped
6 cups chicken stock
1 chicken breast, cooked and diced
¼ pound small meatballs
½ cup *Acini di Pepe* or *Pastina* pasta
1½ cups chopped fresh spinach leaves
Salt and pepper
Parmesan cheese, grated

Heat olive oil in a large pot.
Add garlic and sauté just until garlic is soft and golden.
Add stock and bring to a boil.
Add chicken, meatballs and pasta to pot; cook for 10 minutes.
Add spinach leaves to soup and gently simmer for 3-5 minutes.
Season with salt and pepper, if desired.
Ladle into soup bowls; serve with grated cheese.

White Gazpacho

Bob and Carol Jones ❄ Welch Island

3 medium cucumbers, peeled, seeded and chopped
1-2 cloves garlic, crushed
3 cups chicken broth
3 cups sour cream or Greek-style yogurt
3 tablespoons white vinegar
½ teaspoon salt or to taste

In 3-4 batches, puree cucumbers, garlic, chicken broth, sour cream (or yogurt), vinegar and salt in the blender. Chill several hours.

Garnish with: Diced tomatoes, peppers, red onion or scallions, celery, chopped parsley and *absolutely necessary*…chopped smoked almonds!

Serve with bread.

Hamburger Soup

Norma Keeler ❋ Bear Island

This hearty soup is great for cold weather and freezes well.

¼ cup butter or margarine
1 cup flour
8 cups water
1 pound lean ground beef
1 cup chopped onion
1 cup shredded carrots
1 cup sliced celery
1 can (16-ounce) *Veg-All* or 2 cups frozen mixed vegetables
1 (29-ounce) can tomato sauce or whole tomatoes, un-drained
2 tablespoons granulated beef bouillon
1 teaspoon salt
1 teaspoon ground black pepper

Melt butter in a large soup pot.
Whisk in flour and continue whisking, while you slowly add water until smooth.

Sauté ground beef in a frying pan until well browned; add onions to pan and continue to sauté until translucent. Drain off any excess fat and discard.
Add browned meat to liquid in soup pot.
Stir carrots, celery, mixed vegetables and tomato sauce into beef mixture.
Season with bouillon, salt and pepper.

Bring to a boil, reduce heat and simmer until vegetables are tender.

Serve hot.
Makes 12 servings

❋ ❋ ❋ ❋ ❋

ONLY THE PURE IN HEART CAN MAKE A GOOD SOUP.
Ludwig Van Beethoven

Turkey Vegetable Soup

Evy Chapman ❋ Chase Island

3 carrots, chopped
1 large onion, chopped
2 stalks celery, chopped
½ small turnip, cubed (or parsnips)
3 tablespoons bacon bits
2 cloves garlic, minced
1 (28-ounce) can diced tomatoes with juice
8 cups chicken stock
¼ pound smoked turkey, diced
½ cup uncooked tiny pasta
1 (10-ounce) package frozen chopped spinach, thawed and drained

Spray the bottom of a soup pot with cooking spray.
Add the carrots, onion, celery and turnip.
Cook over low heat, covered, stirring occasionally until carrots and turnip are crisp-tender, about 8-10 minutes.
Add bacon, garlic, tomatoes and stock; bring to a boil.
Add turkey and pasta. Stir until soup returns to a boil.
Cover and cook gently 10 minutes, or until pasta is cooked through.
Add spinach and stir into the hot liquid.
Serve with freshly grated Parmesan cheese and crusty bread.

BEGINNINGS

Treasure Island – Claudette Gammon

We are first-generation islanders, but have been inhabitants of Treasure Island now for nearly 30 years. There are so many stories... from camping with the bats and mice in the original mailroom of Treasure Island's former girls' camp (circa 1950s) – to lugging building supplies out to build the camp – to having our newborn daughter out there before she was two weeks old... living there with her, in September of 1984, until our Manchester home was finished. All are wonderful memories of great times with family and friends!

Our Island is 6-acres in size. We celebrate each summer with an island-wide cocktail party. This has been a tradition now for well over 20 years. We may have missed a couple of years, but we are still trying to keep it strong.

Each family brings an appetizer to share and their own drinks. Children and whatever guests are visiting that day are also invited to attend.

As of now, we intend to remain islanders for quite a while and eventually plan to spend the entire summer out there when we both are fully retired.

Caribbean Coconut Soup

Nanci Stone ❃ Diamond Island

This is a great summer island soup.

1 tablespoon butter or oil
1 large red bell pepper, diced
1 bunch scallions, chopped
1 tablespoon chopped fresh garlic
2 tablespoons grated fresh ginger
2 tablespoons coriander
1 tablespoon curry powder
2 tablespoons sugar
1 teaspoon fresh ground black pepper
1 teaspoon cayenne pepper
2 cans unsweetened coconut milk
4 cups chicken stock
1 can straw mushrooms
2 whole boneless chicken breasts, cooked, cut into ½ inch cubes
1 cup heavy whipping cream

Sauté peppers and scallions in butter until tender; add garlic and cook an additional minute. Sprinkle in ginger, coriander, curry, sugar and peppers. Stir in coconut milk until dissolved.
Add chicken stock, mushrooms and chicken; stir and cook over medium-high heat until it comes to a simmer. Do not boil.
Reduce heat to medium-low; pour heavy cream into soup, stir and heat for an additional 5 minutes.

This is great paired with a Caesar Salad, French bread and well-chilled Chardonnay.

SUNK AT THE DOCK
Diamond Island - Nanci Stone

I watched my new boat -- only 3 hours on the engine -- sink at our dock when a gorgeous Friday afternoon turned into a "Winni-Squall". Sixty-five mile per hour winds blew 5 and 6-foot waves into Diamond Island and the back of my boat-WOW!

GARNASISKA
Mark Island - Glenn Fuller

My grandfather's brother knew my grandfather wanted to name the "fishing camp" on the shores of Winnipesaukee after something native to the area. Somehow he had an affiliation with a couple of Abernaki Indians who knew some of the native language.

They came up with Garnasiska, "a place where the tribe meets for fun and games," which often happened after fishing the "Weirs," as they worked in groups to work the trapping system.

I liked the word, for it's not just one place, it's where the fun and games are.

Some things have not changed over time and it reminds me of today's "work hard and play hard" philosophy. A Garnasiska could happen anywhere!

The name has traveled from my grandfather's fishing camp to my dad's, and now to my place on the island.

Jacqui Jaran and Winni Opel   Photo Courtesy of Glenn Fuller

Bean Pot Stew

Joan Veazey ✳ Mink Island

2 pounds stew beef, cut into bite size pieces
1 large onion, sliced
¼ cup fine bread crumbs
¼ cup tapioca
4 whole cloves garlic
2 teaspoons salt
⅛ teaspoon pepper
1 bunch of carrots, peeled and sliced
1 cup diced tomatoes

Preheat oven to 300°F. Arrange everything in layers in a bean pot, pouring tomatoes over all. Add enough water to cover completely. Cover the pot and place in oven. Bake for 5 hours.

✳ ✳ ✳ ✳ ✳

VEAZEY FAMILY
Mink Island – Joan Veazey

The Veazey family came to Mink Island in approximately 1955. Allen and Nina Veazey came first, followed by John and Bill Veazey and their children, Jane, Sally and Allen, and Suzanne and Chip.

Bill and I built a camp and stayed there most summers. Sue and her children Liza and Hannah came, as did Chip, Joanna, Nick, Chippy, Connor and Sarah.

Long after, our interests changed, and we sold our property to Greg and Joanne Dickinson.

I have many fond memories of good friends and good times on Mink!

Mail Dock on Jolly Island

Hot Diggity Stew

Lauder and Estelle Miller ❄ Jolly Island

This recipe goes back to the days of ice boxes and wood cook stoves; the days when the mail boat stopped twice a day, leaving milk and bread in the morning and taking grocery orders to be filled at Tarlson's at the Weirs and delivered on the afternoon mail boat.
My husband's mother, Grace Stenhouse Miller (1899-1981), was the daughter of Charles Stenhouse – one of the founding ministers of Jolly Island. She was acclaimed by all around her table when she filled their tummies with Hot Diggity Stew.

1⅓ cups water
⅔ cup rice
½ onion, sliced
3-4 hot dogs, sliced
1 (15-ounce) can tomatoes, diced
1 tablespoon sugar

Bring water to a boil. Add rice and cook according to package directions. Sauté onions and hot dogs in a large skillet.
Add cooked rice, tomatoes and sugar. Stir to combine.
Cover and simmer for 15 minutes. Serve with lettuce wedges.

Clam Chowder for Fifty Trekkers

Jim and Cyrene Wells ✳ Mark Island

Between 1967 and 1995 we organized yearly February treks across the barren windswept wastelands of Winnipesaukee, from Cattle Landing to Mark Island. For the most part, the treks were themed—with trophies and ribbon awards. On the "animal" trek, the dogs and horse lost out to two goats.

On arrival at Mark Island, we would shovel snow off the picnic table and out of the fireplace. We would light a fire, add clean snow and a cup of beer to the chowder pot—and cook whatever else the trekkers brought. After lunch, there was often a relay race, followed by the awards ceremony and singing of the Mark Island Navy Trek Anthem.

Night before trek, prepare chowder:

1 pound butter
2½ cups chopped onions
5 cups water
20 cups diced potatoes
15 (6.5-ounce) cans chopped clams (save liquor)
10 (12-ounce) cans evaporated milk
12 tablespoons all-purpose flour
2 tablespoons salt
Pepper to taste
14 ounces dark beer

In a heavy 20-quart pot, melt butter and sauté onion until translucent. Add 5 cups of water, potatoes, onions, and liquor from clams. Cook covered for 15-20 minutes.

Add drained clams. Pour in 9 cans of evaporated milk. Mix the 10th can of evaporated milk with some cold water and blend in flour. Slowly add flour mixture (through a strainer if necessary) into hot chowder. Heat to a gentle boil, stirring constantly. Add salt and pepper to taste.

Put the chowder pot in a cool place until the next day. When transporting the pot, it helps to lay a round board on the top of the chowder to keep it from slopping out from under the lid.

When reheating over an open fire, add a 14-ounce cup of dark draft beer and some clean snow.

Serves 50 (more or less, depending on how cold the weather is, how many hot dogs trekkers have carried along, and how much snow is added).

1992 Ice Trek from Cattle Landing to the Wells' Camp on Mark Island
Photos Courtesy of Jim and Cyrene Wells

ISLAND LIVING - Mark Island - Ray Keating

I am frequently surprised when mainlanders from away ask how we get to our island. We all take the water that surrounds us so much for granted that "by boat" seems like such a silly reply to the question. Over the years the vessels that transport us to our islands have progressed from birch bark canoes to row boats to sailboats, steam boats, and later motor boats.

The evolution of the Mark Island Navy derives from the stubborn resolve of a few people to maintain the tradition of rowing from the mainland to the island. Over time a group of school friends developed a form of a synchronized boating drill, using a small wooden boat with double oar locks. Five members of the Navy, dressed in uniform, would perform a series of maneuvers, such as precision rowing, rapid reverse direction, shipping of oars, presenting of oars, and rapid fire and reloading of cannons. With four members rowing and the coxswain calling out the orders, they would culminate the display by all standing at attention with oars presented, while their ship sank until the surface waters bobbed with 5 sailor hats. A large round of applause from the reviewers standing on the island's shore always followed.

Members of the Mark Island Navy in full uniform re-enact their traditional seamanship drill, complete with bow-mounted cannon and boatswain's piping.

To the command of "Toss---Oars!" the crew demonstrates the precise seamanship it has been long famous for.

Note: Presence of outboard motor precluded the grand finale, sinking of ship.

Like all seafaring people, islanders love food prepared from the bounty of their native waters. My mother-in-law, who did all her island cooking in a fireplace or in the galley of a late 1940's vintage Steelcraft, was a graduate of the Fannie Farmer Boston Cooking School. Here's a recipe from the 9th edition of Fannie's cookbook for Lobster Bisque with an island touch, Lake Winnipesaukee craw fish.

You will need a bait trap, which is a round wire basket with funnel-shaped openings in each end (a little like a lobster trap, only round.) A few days before making this dish, take a fish head or scrap piece of uncooked fish, close it in the trap, and drop it off your dock, secured to the dock with a piece of line. The trap should rest on the bottom close to shore.

Lobster Bisque

Ray Keating ✳ Mark Island

The day you prepare this dish, harvest the craw fish in the trap and toss them into boiling water until they are as red as a lobster. Drain and set aside in the cooler to chill. In the meantime prepare:

2 tablespoons butter
1 teaspoon chopped onion
1 sprig parsley
1½ cups cooked lobster meat, chopped fine
2 tablespoons flour
2 cups chicken stock
2 cups light cream
Salt
Cayenne pepper

In a large soup pot, melt butter and then add onion and parsley.
Cook slowly until onion is yellow. Stir in flour and cook a minute longer.
Add finely-chopped lobster. Cook and stir for 5 minutes.
Add chicken stock and simmer 20 minutes.
Remove parsley.
Add cream and heat without boiling.
Season with salt and cayenne to taste.
Serve the bisque in a shallow soup bowl, placing 2 or 3 of the craw fish around the edge of the bowl for decoration.
(In truth, no one that I know has dared eat the craw fish.)

How to Cook a Lobster:

A lobster will turn bright red before it is thoroughly cooked inside, so to test for doneness, tug on an antenna or pull off one of the small walking legs. Both will come off easily when the lobster is done. Lobster meat should be firm, white and opaque. The tomalley will be a greenish-yellow, and the roe will be a bright orange-red, and firm.

The internal temperature should be 180° F. See chart below for cooking times for boiling or steaming a lobster.

Lobster Weight	Cooking Time
1 - 1 ¼ lb.	12 - 15 minutes
1 ¼ - 2 lb.	15 - 20 minutes
2-3 lb.	20 - 25 minutes
3-6 lb.	25 - 28 minutes
6-7 lb.	28 - 30 minutes
8 lb. and over	4 minutes per pound

Dressed for Dinner

Savory Pies

Spanakopita

Mediterranean Vegetable Pie

Tomato Pie

Sandwiches

Gourmet Grilled Cheese

Muffuletta

Bean Tacos

Pizza

Pantry Pizza

Grill Top Pizza

Deep Cove Pizza Sauce

Make Your Own Pizza

Grilled Caesar Salad Pizza

Spanakopita

Anne Bean ✳ Little Camp Island

A.K.A. Greek Spinach Pie. Although I hate to heat up the kitchen on a hot summer day, this is great to make ahead for company so I'm not cooking when they arrive.

½ cup olive oil
2 large yellow onions, chopped
1 rounded teaspoon parsley
1 rounded teaspoon dill
5 (10-ounce) packages frozen spinach, thawed
4 eggs, beaten
4 ounces small curd cottage cheese
1½ pounds feta cheese, crumbled
1 (1-pound) box filo dough, thawed
10 tablespoons butter, melted

Heat olive oil in large skillet. Add onions, parsley and dill. Sauté until onions are translucent, but not mushy. Set aside.

Squeeze all liquid out of spinach and place in a large mixing bowl with sautéed onion. Mix thoroughly.

In a separate bowl, mix eggs, cottage cheese and most of the feta, until well blended. Add to spinach and mix thoroughly. If you think you want the mixture to be cheesier, add more feta. Set filling aside.

With a pastry brush, butter a 10x15-inch baking pan. Place ten layers of filo dough in the pan, buttering in between each layer, making sure to overlap or stagger sheets in order to achieve complete coverage.

Spread filling mixture evenly onto filo dough without packing it down. Continue with another ten layers of filo over the filling, buttering in between each layer, overlapping for coverage. Roll any overhanging edge of filo around the perimeter and butter well.

Chill in refrigerator for about 15 minutes. Score top layer into desired number of pieces - 6x4 works well.

Preheat oven to 350°F. Bake approximately 45-60 minutes or until filo is a nice golden brown. Cool before cutting. Tastes even better the next day!

✳ ✳ ✳ ✳ ✳

From Wikipedia: **Phyllo, filo,** *or* **fillo** *dough is paper-thin sheets of raw, unleavened flour dough used for making pastries in Middle Eastern, Greek and other regional cuisines.*

Mediterranean Vegetable Pie

Jeannette Buell ✳ Mark Island

From the Rochester, New York, Junior League Applehood and Mother Pie cookbook

1 medium eggplant, peeled and sliced ¼-inch thick
1 teaspoon salt
¾ cup olive oil or vegetable oil
1 large onion, sliced
1 green pepper, cut into thin strips
1 medium zucchini, sliced
2 cloves garlic, minced
¾ teaspoon oregano
¾ teaspoon basil
½ teaspoon salt
½ teaspoon pepper
2 (9-inch) pie crusts, unbaked
½ cup grated Parmesan cheese
2 medium tomatoes, seeded and cut into eighths
8-ounces shredded Mozzarella cheese
1 tablespoon milk

Sprinkle eggplant slices with salt and place between paper towels. Weight down with heavy cutting board for 30 minutes.

Heat ½ cup of the oil in a skillet. Cut eggplant slices into cubes. Add to hot oil, toss. Cook until tender, stirring constantly (about 5 minutes). Remove eggplant and set aside.

Pour remaining oil into skillet. Add onion, green pepper, zucchini and garlic. Cook just until tender (about 5 minutes).

Combine spices and salt. Set aside.

Line a 9-inch pie plate with pastry. Sprinkle with ¼ cup of the Parmesan cheese. Spoon half the eggplant and half the vegetable mixture into pie shell. Layer with half of the tomato wedges, half of the spice mixture, and half of the Mozzarella cheese. Repeat these layers. Sprinkle top with all but 1 tablespoon of Parmesan cheese.

Make a lattice-top crust by crossing strips of dough one over the other. Sprinkle with milk and remaining 1 tablespoon of the Parmesan cheese.

Bake in a preheated oven at 425°F. for 25 minutes. Let stand for 15 minutes before cutting.

Tomato Pie

Daryl Thompson ❋ Welch Island

Courtesy of our friend, Mary Ann Limric, former resident of Lockes Island

1 (9-inch) pie crust
4 medium ripe tomatoes, peeled, sliced ½ inch thick, drained on paper towels
¼ cup chopped chives or scallions
1-3 tablespoons chopped fresh basil
¼ teaspoon fresh ground black pepper
¼ teaspoon salt
1½ cups grated Swiss cheese
¼ to ½ cup mayonnaise

Preheat oven to 425°F. Line a 9" pie plate with crust and bake for 5 minutes. Remove from oven.

Reduce heat to 400°F. Place tomato slices on bottom of baked shell. Sprinkle tomatoes with chives, basil, salt and pepper.

Combine cheese and mayonnaise. Spread mixture evenly over tomatoes, making sure it reaches the edges of pie crust and seals in the tomatoes.

Bake pie 30-35 minutes or until brown and bubbly.
Allow pie to cool 5-10 minutes before cutting. Serve warm.

Gourmet Grilled Cheese Sandwiches

Lisa Rich Libby ❋ Mark Island

These were often made after crossing the lake on dark and stormy nights.
My Dad enjoyed his with Balentine Ale while Mom and I preferred champagne.

1 loaf hearty Jewish rye bread with seeds, sliced thick
Butter
Garlic powder or parslied garlic salt
Sliced Jarlsburg Swiss cheese or American
Honey baked ham or deli honey-maple ham, optional

Butter sliced bread and season to taste.
Fill with cheese and ham.
Heat cast-iron skillet or non-stick pan.
Grill the sandwich until golden brown on both sides.

Note: Peruse the refrigerator, for different "fillers." Create new favorites....try rare roast beef instead of ham and toss in a bit of horseradish for some kick.

Muffuletta

Bill Buell ✳ Mark Island

What makes this sandwich special is the olive salad. You will want to make it an hour or two before eating, so the juices can soak into the bread. This is the perfect picnic sandwich.

Olive Salad:
4 celery ribs, finely chopped
1 cup drained giardiniera (pickled vegetables), finely chopped
1 cup loosely packed fresh parsley, chopped
¾ cup pitted green olives, finely chopped
¼ cup olive oil
¼ teaspoon coarse ground black pepper
1 garlic clove, minced
½ teaspoon celery seed

1 round loaf of soft French or Italian bread cut horizontally in half (10-inch diameter, about 1 pound)

¼ pound sliced mortadella
¼ pound sliced capicola ham
¼ pound sliced provolone cheese
¼ pound thinly sliced Genoa salami

In a medium bowl, combine celery, giardiniera, parsley, olives, olive oil, black pepper, garlic and celery seed. Set aside.

Remove a 1" layer of soft center of bread from both halves, to make room for the filling. On bottom half of bread, spread half of the olive salad; top with mortadella, ham, cheese, salami, and remaining olive salad. Replace the top of the bread and press halves together.

Wrap sandwich tightly in plastic wrap, then in foil.
Refrigerate with something heavy set on top for at least 2 hours or up to 24 hours.

Cut into 8 wedges and serve.

Bean Tacos

Barbara Whetstone ✳ Treasure Island

Quick, easy and the kids love them!
Add meat, vegetables and additional salsa, if you wish.

1 cup water
1 (12-ounce) can baked beans
¼ cup salsa
¾ cup couscous, any flavor

One large box Taco shells
1 cup grated cheese, Monterey Jack or Cheddar

Preheat oven or toaster oven to 350°F.

Put the water, beans, salsa and couscous in a sauce pan. Bring to a boil, and then remove from heat. Stir and cover. Let stand for 5 minutes. Stir again.

Stuff each taco shell, leaving room to insert some cheese.

Arrange filled tacos on a baking sheet. Warm in the oven until the cheese has melted.

Pantry Pizza

Joanne Moulton ✳ Sleeper Island

Make a baking powder or *Jiffy Mix* crust.
Find any leftovers in the refrigerator for toppings.
Sprinkle with cheese.
Finish with fresh or dried herbs.
Bake according to crust instructions.

Grill-Top Pizza

Claudette Gammon ❋ Treasure Island

I usually start the season with pizza dough in the freezer.

1 pizza dough, fresh or frozen
Olive oil
Pizza sauce
Favorite toppings from your refrigerator
Mozzarella cheese
Grated Parmesan or Asiago cheese

Sauté or microwave your toppings until tender: onion, garlic, and leftover vegetables, such as broccoli, peppers and tomatoes. Season to taste with salt and pepper.

Roll or press out thawed pizza dough. Lightly brush both sides of dough with olive oil and place on an oiled cookie sheet with no sides.

Heat the grill to medium-high.

Slide the pressed-out pizza dough onto the grill.

Cook for 3 to 5 minutes, and then turn it over.

Once it's turned, spread the pizza sauce on the dough, top with vegetables and sliced or shredded mozzarella cheese. Sprinkle the shredded Parmesan cheese over all.

Cook until cheese is melted, being careful not to let the dough burn.

Note: Put the grill cover down, but don't walk away. Watch pizza closely.

Another variation:
Think Greek... brush olive oil on the dough, then top with sliced tomatoes, olives, basil and feta cheese.

❋ ❋ ❋ ❋ ❋

Tip for reheating leftover pizza:
To keep the crust crispy, heat pizza slices in a nonstick skillet on top of the stove. Set temperature to medium-low and heat until warm.

Deep Cove Pizza Sauce

Sharon Doyle ❋ Bear Island

This is Mama Taranto's pizza sauce. Make a big batch to freeze. This is also good with Parmesan recipes.

Basic Pizza Sauce:
2 tablespoons olive oil
4 cloves crushed garlic
2 (8-ounce) cans tomato sauce, unflavored
½ cup water
2 teaspoons dried oregano
1 teaspoon dried basil
Salt and pepper

Sauté garlic cloves in oil until soft.

Add tomato sauce, water, oregano, basil, salt and pepper.

Cook over medium heat for 5-10 minutes.

Pizza:

Pizza dough, pre-made

Roll or press dough (patted thin) on an oiled baking tray.
Spread dough with pizza sauce.

Add toppings of your choice: cooked sausage, sautéed mushrooms, diced sautéed peppers, basil leaves, and so on.

Cover with shredded mozzarella cheese.
Bake at 450-500°F. until cheese is bubbling and bottom of crust is done.

❋ ❋ ❋ ❋ ❋

Tip: If you like your crust crunchy, try sprinkling a little cornmeal on the oiled baking pan before putting the crust on the pan.

Make~Your~Own~Pizza

Kathleen Aceto ❋ Welch Island

Last minute pizza dough:
2 cups very warm water
2 (.25 ounce) packages dry yeast
5¼ cups flour
1 teaspoon salt
½ teaspoon olive oil

Mix ingredients. Knead for 5 minutes.
Place in a greased bowl and cover with towel.
Place in oven that has been warmed to 200°F. **then turned off.**
Let rise 20 minutes.

Pizza sauce:
1 (29-ounce) can tomato sauce
1 (6-ounce) can tomato paste
1 teaspoon oregano
1 teaspoon basil
Pinch of sugar
Pinch of hot pepper flakes

Simmer all sauce ingredients together in a pan for 15-20 minutes. Cool.

Once the dough has risen, divide it into 3 portions.
Stretch or roll into 3 crusts.

Preheat oven to 450°F.
Place dough onto oiled baking sheets or pizza pans.
Spread sauce onto the prepared dough.
Top with your favorite combination of toppings: sausage, pepperoni, mushrooms, red peppers, mozzarella…etc.

Position pan in the lower portion of the oven. Bake, one pizza at a time, until the crust is browned and the toppings are warmed and melted.

Note: For a crispier crust, about 5 minutes before the end of the baking time, slide crust from pan and let pizza finish cooking on the oven rack.

Grilled Caesar Salad Pizza

Debbie Kennedy ❋ Rattlesnake Island

This makes a great appetizer or meal.

1 pizza dough ball
1 (4-ounce) package *Boursin* cheese (or *Pub* cheese)
Grilled shrimp or cooked, sliced chicken, optional
1 package shredded pizza cheese, divided

Romaine lettuce, cleaned and torn
Croutons
Creamy Caesar salad dressing

Warm pizza dough to room temperature.
Sprinkle dough with flour and pull into a rectangle.
Transfer to an oiled baking sheet.

Preheat grill; oil grates.
Slide the pizza dough onto the grill; close the cover and cook until the bottom of crust is firm and browned (check after 2 minutes). Flip crust over and cook for just one more minute.

Slide crust back onto the baking sheet.
Spread with *Boursin* cheese, and add shrimp or chicken. Sprinkle with ⅔ of the pizza cheese.

Slide pizza back onto the grill, and heat until the toppings are warmed and melted.

Remove from the grill to a cutting board. Slice pizza into desired number of slices.

Top pizza with lettuce and croutons, and drizzle with dressing. Sprinkle with remaining pizza cheese.

Serve immediately.

Kalee, Abby, Jesse and Becky Thompson

Potato

Sweet Potato Salad

Deli Potato Salad

Pasta

Orzo Salad

Pepperoni Pasta Salad

Thai Pasta Salad

Fruit

Pineapple Summer Salad

Ambrosia

Vegetable

Summer Corn Salad

Uncle Bill's Cucumber Salad

Pea-Lover Salad

Fresh Broccoli Salad

Mixed Vegetable Salad

Grains and Beans

Four Bean Salad

Tabouli Salad

Rice and Black Bean Salad

Leafy Greens

4th of July Mink Island Salad

Mark Island Caesar Salad

Barndoor Caesar Salad

Cobb Salad

Mandarin Salad

Spinach Strawberry Salad

Little Bear Berry Salad

Lockes Island Spinach Salad

Salad of Love

Slaw

Little Bear Crunchy Cole Slaw

Mink Island Cole Slaw

Six-Week Cole Slaw

Chicken

Kee-Ting-Bong-Bong Salad

Curried Chicken Salad

Leftover Chicken Salad

Dressings

Dolly Island Vinaigrette

Blue Cheese Dressing

Creamy Garlic Vinaigrette

Poppy Seed Dressing

Orzo Salad

Kathleen Aceto ✳ Welch Island

½ (16-ounce) box orzo, cooked, drained and rinsed with cold water
½ pound snow peas, trimmed and blanched
3 scallions, chopped
1 yellow pepper, seeded and chopped
1 cucumber, peeled, seeded and chopped
1 cup crumbled feta cheese
½ cup toasted pine nuts
¼ cup olive oil
¼ cup vegetable oil
⅓ cup vinegar (either balsamic or raspberry)
1 clove garlic, minced
Salt and pepper to taste

In a large bowl, combine orzo, snow peas, scallions, pepper, cucumbers, feta, and nuts.
In a small bowl, whisk together oils, vinegar, garlic, salt and pepper.
Pour dressing over salad and toss well.

Pepperoni Pasta Salad

Rick and Karen Dean ✳ Lockes Island

1 pound penne pasta, cooked and drained
1 green pepper, chopped
½ cup sliced and chopped pepperoni
1 teaspoon garlic powder
1 bottle *Good Seasons* Italian dressing (prepared according to package directions)
Salt and pepper to taste

In a large bowl combine the cooked pasta, green pepper, pepperoni, garlic powder and Italian dressing. Toss to coat. Chill until ready to serve.

Thai Pasta Salad

Abby Thompson ❋ Welch Island

1 package (1 pound) thin spaghetti

Dressing:
3 tablespoons chunky peanut butter
5 tablespoons salad oil
¼ cup soy sauce
¼ cup sugar
1 teaspoon sesame oil
4 teaspoons white vinegar
1 teaspoon hot chili oil
2 teaspoons ginger, minced
2 cloves garlic, minced
Red pepper flakes to taste

2 tablespoon green onion, minced
2 tablespoons fresh cilantro, chopped

Boil, drain and rinse spaghetti with cool water.

Blend all dressing ingredients together in large bowl. Add cooled noodles to dressing; toss to coat.
Top with green onions and cilantro.

Grilled chicken can be added if desired.

Guarding the Tent   Photo Courtesy of Brian Carroll

Pineapple Summer Salad

Roxane Gwyn ❈ Cow Island

I've had great fun working in the kitchen with nieces and nephews of all ages to create this family favorite. The presentation is dramatic!

Dressing:
2 cloves garlic, minced
1 red chili pepper, seeded and minced
1 tablespoon soy sauce
Juice of ½ lime (about 1 tablespoon)
2 teaspoons brown sugar

Salad:
1½ cups fresh pineapple chunks
2 medium cucumbers cut into chunks
3 spring onions, sliced
1 red bell pepper, thinly sliced
½ cup whole roasted unsalted cashews
1 cup fresh basil, roughly chopped
1 cup fresh cilantro, roughly chopped

Preparation:
Combine all dressing ingredients in a cup, stir well, and set aside.
Place all salad ingredients into a mixing bowl, setting aside a little cilantro and cashews for garnish.
Pour dressing over salad just before serving, no earlier, and be sure not to over-dress. Toss well.

Serving option: Scoop salad into hollowed-out pineapple boats on large, individual serving plates. Top with extra cilantro and nuts, and put a couple of lime wedges on each plate.

From Wikipedia:
Shopping for pineapple: Look for a pineapple that is golden-yellow in color. Never buy a green pineapple, as pineapples do not ripen well after harvesting. Pineapples should smell sweet. If there is no scent, it's not ripe. If it smells fermented, it has gone beyond ripe. A fresh pineapple should yield only slightly to gentle pressure. If it feels soft, it is over-ripe.

Ambrosia

Nelson and Jan Maynard ❋ Welch Island

1 (20-ounce) can pineapple chunks, drained
1 (11-ounce) can Mandarin oranges, drained
1 banana, peeled and sliced
1½ cup seedless grapes, halved
1½ cup miniature marshmallows
½ cup shredded coconut
¼ cup slivered almonds
1 (8-ounce) carton vanilla yogurt

Combine the first seven ingredients.
Fold in yogurt. Chill well.

Summer Corn Salad

Kathleen Aceto ❋ Welch Island

Or what to do with left over corn-on-the-cob…

3-4 ears of corn, grilled or steamed, with corn cut off the cob
1 pound green beans, cooked crisp and cooled
1½ cups cherry tomatoes, halved
⅓ cup fresh basil, chopped
3 tablespoons chopped red onion
1 (15-ounce) can black beans, drained and rinsed

Customize this salad with other seasonal vegetables, toasted walnuts, or crumbled cheeses.

Vinaigrette:
½ cup vegetable oil
⅓ cup balsamic or raspberry vinegar
Salt and pepper
1 teaspoon Dijon mustard, optional

Combine prepared vegetables, basil and beans in a salad bowl. Toss with vinaigrette. Refrigerate until ready to serve.

Uncle Bill's Cucumber Salad

Jane Veasey MacFadzen ❋ Mink Island

Born and raised on the "Big Lake," my first summer baby pictures are at the age of six months and were taken on Lockes Island. Moving over to Mink Island to Buttercup's (a name my Grandfather called Nana) at the other end of Mink, my Uncle Bill was known for his cuisine, as well as Bloody Marys. Word would spread thru-out the islands like wild fire that "the Mayor of Mink" was cooking. My favorite was his cucumber salad.

Thinly slice cucumbers...as many as you have on hand, which is usually a lot! Place slices in a bowl of ice-cold salted water...as fast as the ice melts throw more ice in. Slice up white onions and toss in the ice water...sit and wait. Have a Bloody Mary.

Take a bottle of white vinegar, and pour into a separate bowl. Mix some sugar into the vinegar…sweet/sour. Adjust to your taste buds.

Drain cucumbers and onions. Pour vinegar mixture over the vegetables. Place in refrigerator.

Enjoy with baked beans. This salad will last for awhile ...but it usually doesn't.

Pea~Lover Salad

Connie Grant ❋ Welch Island

1 (2-pound) bag of frozen peas, thawed
¼ cup peanuts, crushed
¼ cup macadamia nuts, coarsely chopped
1 cup sour cream
2~3 tablespoons soy sauce
2~3 green onions, thinly sliced

Set peas aside in colander for thawing about ½ hour before preparation or rinse with cold water if time is an issue.

Put peanuts in a plastic bag and crush to a fine texture.
Put macadamia nuts in a plastic bag and crush to a coarse texture.

In a large mixing bowl, blend together sour cream and soy sauce. Add prepared peas, green onions, and nuts. Toss to coat.

Refrigerate until ready to serve.

Fresh Broccoli Salad

Daryl Thompson ✻ Welch Island

1 head broccoli, cut into bite size florets
1 pound bacon, cooked crisp and crumbled
½ cup raisins or dried cranberries
½ cup sesame seeds
1 cup mayonnaise
½ cup sugar
2 tablespoons vinegar

In a large bowl, combine broccoli, bacon, raisins and sesame seeds.
In a separate bowl, combine mayonnaise, sugar and vinegar.
Whisk together. Pour dressing over broccoli and toss to coat.
Chill salad for several hours or overnight.

Mixed Vegetable Salad

Carmel Hanson ✻ Bear Island

Feel free to substitute your favorite fresh and canned vegetables to suit your tastes.

Dressing:
⅔ cup vegetable oil
½ cup sugar
½ cup white vinegar
2 teaspoons dry mustard
2 teaspoons salt

1 (15.5-ounce) can whole kernel corn, drained
1 (8-ounce) sliced water chestnuts, drained and cut in half
1 large onion, chopped
1 cup sliced celery
½ head cauliflower, cut into florets
½ head broccoli, cut into florets
1 red pepper, chopped
1 green pepper, chopped

In a jar with a tight fitting cover, combine oil, sugar, vinegar, dry mustard and
salt. Cover, shake vigorously and set aside.
In a large bowl, combine corn, water chestnuts, onion, celery, cauliflower,
broccoli and peppers. Pour dressing mixture over vegetables and toss to coat.
Cover and refrigerate. During the chilling process, stir a couple of times.
When ready to serve, toss to coat once more.

Four-Bean Salad

Nancy L. Buell ❋ Mark Island

Dressing:
¾ cup cider vinegar
¼ cup water

½ cup olive oil
½-1 cup sugar
Salt and pepper

1 (15-ounce) can baby Lima beans
1 (14.5-ounce) can wax-cut beans
1 (14.5-ounce) can French-cut green beans
1 (15-ounce) can kidney beans, drained and rinsed
1 medium red onion, sliced thin
1 green or red pepper, seeded and sliced thin

Whisk together dressing ingredients.
Drain and rinse beans well. Combine beans, onion and pepper with dressing,
tossing well to coat. Cover and refrigerate overnight.

Tabouli Salad

Patti Bezanson Fielding ❋ Little Bear Island

1 (5.25-ounce) box of Tabouli mix
1 (6-ounce) small jar of marinated artichoke hearts, chopped (reserve marinade
when draining)
1 (15.5-ounce) can of dark red kidney beans, drained
½ cup chopped sun-dried tomatoes
2 plum tomatoes, chopped
1 cucumber, chopped
1 yellow bell pepper, chopped
1 small red onion, chopped
1 handful of cilantro, chopped
2 cloves of garlic, minced
1 lemon, juiced
3 tablespoons olive oil
Salt and pepper to taste

Make the Tabouli mix as directed. Let it cool.
In a large bowl, combine Tabouli, artichokes, kidney beans, tomatoes, sun dried
tomatoes, cucumber, bell pepper, onion, cilantro and garlic. Toss to mix.
In a small bowl, combine lemon juice, olive oil and the 3 tablespoons of
marinade from the artichokes.
Whisk to blend and season with salt and pepper.
Pour dressing over salad ingredients. Mix well.

Rice and Black Bean Salad

Mary Jo Ray ❋ Rattlesnake Island

We like this easy 'island style' recipe so much that we made it for our daughter's wedding weekend celebration, August 12, 2006. Friends and family gathered at our cottage to celebrate the wedding of Gina and Ben. With the wind blowing and sun shining, vows were recited with the lake behind the couple.

Vinaigrette:
6 tablespoons white wine vinegar
4 teaspoons coarse grain Dijon mustard
2 teaspoons ground cumin
1 teaspoon salt
½ teaspoon black pepper
1 cup olive oil
½ teaspoon hot pepper sauce

Salad:
2~3 cups cooked long grain rice, cooled
1 (15-ounce) can black beans, drained and rinsed
1~2 cups seeded and diced plum tomatoes
1 green pepper, seeded and cut into ½ inch chunks
½ cup coarsely chopped red onion

To make vinaigrette:
Combine the vinegar, mustard, cumin, salt and pepper in a small bowl. Whisk in the olive oil, and then the hot pepper sauce.

For the salad:
Combine the rice, beans, tomatoes, bell pepper and onion in large bowl. Add the vinaigrette and mix well.

Let stand about 30 minutes at room temperature or up to 3 hours in the refrigerator before serving.

Serves at least 6.

❋ ❋ ❋ ❋ ❋

THE GOOD LIFE IS ONE INSPIRED BY LOVE AND GUIDED BY KNOWLEDGE. Bertrand Russell

4th of July Mink Island Salad

Becky Wright ✳ Mink Island

Dressing:
¾ cup olive oil
⅓ cup sugar
¼ cup red wine vinegar
1 tablespoon soy sauce

½ cup butter, cubed
1 tablespoon sugar
2 packages (3-ounces each) Raman noodles, crushed
⅓ cup sesame seeds
¼ cup silvered almonds

2 heads romaine lettuce, washed, dried and torn
4 green onions, thinly sliced

In a jar with tight-fitting lid, combine the dressing ingredients. Shake well. Chill until ready to serve.

In a large skillet, melt butter and sugar over medium heat. Add the noodles, sesame seeds and almonds. (Discard seasoning packets from noodles.) Cook and stir for 6-8 minutes or until browned. Set aside.

In a large salad bowl, toss the romaine and onions.

Just before serving, drizzle salad dressing over romaine mixture and top with noodle mixture. Toss to coat.

12 servings

✳ ✳ ✳ ✳ ✳

IT'S ALWAYS GOOD TO REMEMBER WHERE YOU COME FROM AND CELEBRATE IT. TO REMEMBER WHERE YOU COME FROM IS PART OF WHERE YOU'RE GOING. Anthony Burgess

Mark Island Caesar Salad

Jill Billings Buell ❋ Mark Island

Croutons:
3 tablespoons olive oil
2-4 cloves garlic, minced
4 slices of light and dark breads, toasted, cut into cubes

Combine oil and garlic. Let stand for at least 30 minutes. Remove garlic from oil. Mix flavored oil with toast cubes just before tossing salad.

Dressing:
2 lemons, juiced
⅓ cup olive oil
⅓ cup *Kraft* grated Parmesan cheese
1 egg, beaten

Salt and pepper to taste
1 ready-to-eat bag romaine lettuce

Whisk together lemon juice, olive oil, Parmesan cheese, egg, salt and pepper. Toss with lettuce and prepared croutons.

Make salad at least 30 minutes before serving.

❋ ❋ ❋ ❋ ❋

SHARED EXPERIENCES
Barndoor Island – Jenni Gemberling

We have been Barndoor residents since 1999 and have summered on Winnipesaukee for years. Now the summer experiences that my sister and I had are shared by our boys- summer jobs in Wolfeboro, sailing, swimming and other water activities.

Our cottage is rustic and pretty much technology free—save the $2 TV — which Tucker purchased at the street fair because he lamented, "It was cheaper than the lemonade."

Barndoor Caesar Salad

Jenny Gemberling ❄ Barndoor Island

1 large head of romaine lettuce, cleaned and torn
Croutons

Dressing:
1 clove garlic, minced or pressed
½ cup olive oil
¼ cup fresh squeezed lemon juice
1 tablespoon Worcestershire sauce
1 beaten egg
1 can anchovy filets, whole or minced
1 cup grated Asiago cheese
Salt and pepper to taste

For dressing, combine oil and garlic. Let rest for 30 minutes if possible.
Blend in lemon juice, Worcestershire sauce, beaten egg and anchovy filets. Stir
in ½ cup Asiago cheese.
Toss dressing with prepared lettuce and croutons. Sprinkle remaining cheese on
top.

Cobb Salad

Brad Thompson ❄ Welch Island

1½ heads iceberg lettuce, shredded
4 cups chopped cooked chicken
4 hard-cooked eggs, peeled and chopped
3 tomatoes, seeded and chopped
1 cup crumbled blue cheese
10 slices bacon, cooked crisp and crumbled
2 avocados, peeled, pitted and diced
4 green onions, chopped
12-ounces bottled ranch salad dressing-or your favorite

Divide shredded lettuce evenly between 6 serving plates. Continue dividing and
layering ingredients in the order listed.
Drizzle with your favorite salad dressing.

Mandarin Salad

Carmel Hanson ❊ Bear Island

This is a great do-ahead recipe.

1 cup sliced almonds
⅓ cup sugar

½ cup vegetable or olive oil
5 tablespoons white vinegar
4 tablespoons sugar
2 tablespoons chopped fresh parsley
1 teaspoon salt
Dash pepper
¼ teaspoon red pepper sauce

10 cups assorted loose leaf lettuces, washed, dried, torn into bite-size pieces
4 stalks celery, chopped
5 green onions, thinly sliced
2 (11-ounce) cans mandarin orange segments, drained

Combine almonds and sugar in a one-quart pan over low heat, stirring constantly until sugar is melted and almonds are coated. Turn out onto waxed paper. Cool and break apart.
(Store almonds at room temperature up to one week.)

In a jar with a tight fitting lid, combine oil, vinegar, sugar, parsley, salt, pepper and pepper sauce. Cover and shake well. This may be refrigerated for up to one week.

In a large resealable plastic bag, combine prepared lettuces, celery and green onion. This will hold in the refrigerator for up to 24 hours.

Just before serving, add dressing and oranges to bag. Reseal and shake well to coat.

Turn salad into a serving bowl. Sprinkle with almonds.

Lockes Island Spinach Salad

Dot Pangburn ✳ Lockes Island

Dressing:
1 cup vegetable oil
¾ cup cider vinegar
1 tablespoon soy sauce
½ cup sugar
¾ cup chili sauce

2 pounds spinach, washed and dried
1 medium red onion, cut in rings
4 hard-cooked eggs, peeled and sliced
4 slices bacon, cooked and crumbled
¼ cup sliced almonds (optional)

To make the dressing, combine oil, vinegar, soy sauce, sugar and chili sauce. Chill.

When ready to serve, choose your favorite salad bowl and pour dressing over the prepared spinach, tossing to coat.
Arrange onions, eggs and bacon on top of dressed spinach.
Sprinkle the top with almonds, if desired.

Salad of Love

Anne Hummel ✳ Mark Island

Our friends Tony and Kate, aboard the Sirena at Fay's Boat Yard, shared this special salad with us.

1 package baby spinach, cleaned
1 quart fresh strawberries, hulled and sliced
½ cup smoked almonds, chopped
4 ounces blue cheese, crumbled
3 parts extra virgin olive oil
1 part balsamic vinegar
Sea salt and black pepper

In your favorite salad bowl, top spinach with strawberries, nuts and cheese. Combine oil and vinegar, season to taste. Dress salad, toss and enjoy!

Little Bear Crunchy Cole Slaw

Barbara Cohen ❋ Little Bear Island

½ cup slivered almonds
1 teaspoon butter
1 (16-ounce) package chopped coleslaw
1 tablespoon finely chopped onion
1 package *Ramen* oriental beef noodle soup (break up noodles)

Dressing:
½ cup sugar
½ cup red wine vinegar
⅓ cup vegetable oil
¼ teaspoon salt
Beef seasoning packet from *Ramen* noodles

Sauté almonds in butter until lightly browned.
Combine salad ingredients. Toss with dressing just before serving.

Mink Island Cole Slaw

Steve and Sue Cutillo ❋ Mink Island

I remember helping my grandmother make this when I was a little girl. She would cut the cabbage and I would operate the vegetable peeler. The ingredients were always the same, but the amounts would vary according to mood and availability. It's a perfect recipe for the island. The vegetables can be grown in the garden and the leftovers can return to the garden by way of the mulch pile. And even a small child can operate a vegetable peeler and a large spoon!

1 head of cabbage, shredded
4-5 carrots, peeled and sliced thin
1-2 green peppers, cut into thin strips
6-8 sweet gherkins, chopped
½ cup mayonnaise
¼ cup juice from sweet gherkins

Combine prepared vegetables in a large bowl and toss. Moisten with mayonnaise. Pour pickle juice over all and mix well. Keep refrigerated.

Six-Week Cole Slaw

Dot Pangburn ✳ Lockes Island

1 3-pound head of cabbage, finely chopped or shredded
2 cups water
1 cup sugar
1 cup vinegar
1 teaspoon salt
1 teaspoon celery seed, optional

In a medium saucepan, bring water and sugar to a boil, cooking until a fine thread forms when dropped from a spoon - or until it registers 230°F. on a candy thermometer.
Stir in vinegar, salt and celery seed, if desired. Cool completely.
Pour dressing over cabbage and mix well. Keep refrigerated.
Keeps for 6 weeks! Makes 16 cups.

WEDDING GIFT
Lockes Island - Dave and Dot Pangburn

During WWI a young Laconia man came to Harrington Park, New Jersey, to board at the home of Mr. and Mrs. Wilson and their daughter Muriel, while he worked at the Brooklyn Navy Yard. He told the Wilson family of the wonders of New Hampshire, specifically the mountains and Lake Winnipesaukee.

In the summer of 1920 or so, the Wilsons, their daughter Muriel and her friend Hazel Wygant, spent several weeks at the Winnicoet Hotel in the Weirs.

They liked the locale so well, they then rented a camp on Lockes Island. Soon the Wilsons and Hazel and her fiancé, Sheldon Pangburn, decided to buy 800 feet on the southwest shore of Lockes Island.

Sheldon built the camp as a wedding gift for his bride. Muriel and Hazel brought all the lumber over from shore and Sheldon built the camp, with the help of a local carpenter. Imagine sawing all that wood by hand!

The Pangburns then spent their honeymoon there. The family has spent every summer there since 1926, carefully saving gas coupons during the war years for the trip.

Improvements have been made: electricity in 1947, a bathroom in 1961, a dishwasher in 1971 and a computer in 2002.

House-of Kee-Ting-Bong-Bong-Chicken
Ray Keating ※ Mark Island

Great for a hot summer night! This one doesn't even require a Wok, but it may require a boat trip to the grocery store...

2 chicken breasts
1 head iceberg lettuce
1 scallion, chopped
4 to 6 slices of peeled fresh ginger, shredded
1 tablespoon light soy sauce
2 tablespoons creamy peanut butter
1 tablespoon vinegar
1½ teaspoons sugar
1½ teaspoons salt, divided
¼ to ½ teaspoon sesame oil

2 tablespoons peanut oil (do not substitute)
¼ teaspoon cayenne pepper or 1 tablespoon red pepper flakes

Chop Sticks, optional

Rub chicken with 1 teaspoon salt, place on a plate, and steam in a steamer for 15 minutes, covered. Allow to cool thoroughly. (If bone in, and/or with skin, remove bones and/or skin.)

Shred lettuce (not too small) and spread evenly on a serving platter. Tear chicken into long, thin strips and distribute on top of the lettuce.

Mix scallion, ginger, soy sauce, peanut butter, vinegar, sugar, ½ teaspoon salt, and sesame oil together.

Heat peanut oil in a small sauce pan until very hot –until almost smoking. Add hot pepper to hot oil and immediately remove from heat.

Stir in the ginger-soy mixture. Blend until peanut butter is melted.
Drizzle over the chicken/lettuce base and serve immediately.

Curried Chicken Salad

Mary and Harold Dexter ❋ Welch Island

U.S. Senator J.W. Fulbright, a frequent summer visitor of the Welch Island Donskers, was our guest for lunch and as no opossum was available, we served chicken salad in a honeydew melon - with island-grown tomatoes.

8 cups cooked chicken, cubed
1 (8-ounce) can water chestnuts, drained and sliced
2 pounds seedless grapes, halved
2-3 cups celery, sliced
2 ½ cups sliced almonds, divided
3 cups mayonnaise
1 tablespoon curry powder
2 tablespoons soy sauce
2 tablespoons lemon juice

Combine chicken, water chestnuts, grapes, celery and 1½ cups sliced almonds. In a separate bowl, mix mayonnaise, curry powder, soy sauce and lemon juice. Add dressing to chicken mixture and toss well. Chill several hours. Sprinkle with remaining almonds before serving.

Leftover Chicken Salad

Amelia Welt Katzen ❋ Dolly Island

The beauty of cooking too much food is of course the great things you get to do with the leftovers. The Cilantro Chicken makes a great chicken salad on the 'morrow. We like to add whatever other leftovers there might be—the salsa, vegetables (broccoli, snow peas, peas, corn, tomatoes, avocado), pasta or rice—and then add a simple vinaigrette. Fruit (apples, peaches, grapes) can also liven up the dish.

Chicken, cooked and cubed

Only limited by your imagination… use what you have that you think would be delicious with chicken.

Toss with the appropriate amount of Dolly Island Vinaigrette - recipe follows.

Dolly Island Vinaigrette

Amelia Welt Katzen ❉ Dolly Island

This recipe relies on your tasting the dressing to adjust the various ingredients. As my grandmother would say, you need a philanthropist for the oil, a miser for the vinegar, and a crazy man ("un fou") for the mixing. Double or triple this recipe as necessary for the amount of salad you are making.

Vinaigrette:
6 tablespoons safflower, canola or corn oil
3 tablespoons red wine vinegar
5-10 shakes salt
25 grinds of fresh ground black pepper
¼ teaspoon garlic powder
1 teaspoon mayonnaise
1 tablespoon chopped fresh parsley
1 tablespoon minced onion (optional)

Combine all ingredients in a jar with a tight-fitting lid. Shake well. Refrigerate until needed.

Blue Cheese Dressing

Thelma Malafey ❉ Welch Island

¾ cup sour cream
½ teaspoon dry mustard
½ teaspoon black pepper
½ teaspoon salt, scant
⅓ teaspoon garlic powder, scant
1 teaspoon Worcestershire sauce
1⅓ cups mayonnaise
4 ounces Danish blue cheese, crumbled

In a mixing bowl, combine sour cream, dry mustard, pepper, salt, garlic powder and Worcestershire sauce. Blend 2 minutes at low speed with an electric mixer.

Add mayonnaise and blend ½ minute at low speed, then increase speed to medium and blend an additional 2 minutes.

Slowly add blue cheese and blend at low speed - no longer than 4 minutes. Refrigerate for 24 hours before serving. Yield: 2½ cups

Creamy Garlic Vinaigrette

Margot McKean ❋ Mark Island

¼ cup olive oil
2 tablespoons sour cream
1 tablespoon white wine vinegar
1 tablespoon fresh lemon juice
2 teaspoons Dijon-style mustard
1 garlic clove, minced
¼ teaspoon salt
Fresh ground black pepper to taste

Combine all ingredients in a jar with a tight-fitting lid, or small plastic container. Seal lid, and shake vigorously - about 20 seconds.

This dressing is great with red and green leaf lettuce or a mix of spring greens. Caution: do not over dress because this is a strong dressing.

Poppy Seed Dressing

Jeannette Buell ❋ Mark Island

This recipe came from our friend Ellen Guigere, the original owner of Laconia Village Bakery. This dressing created the sweet and tangy magic in her tortellini pasta salad. Thank you, Ellen, for sharing your magic with us.

1½ cups sugar
2 teaspoons dry mustard
2 teaspoons salt
⅔ cup cider vinegar
2 cups vegetable oil
3 tablespoons poppy seeds

Combine the sugar, dry mustard, salt and vinegar in a blender or food processor. Blend until the sugar is dissolved.

Slowly add the oil while the machine is running, blending until thick and emulsified. Stir in the poppy seeds.

This dressing keeps almost indefinitely in the refrigerator.

Use this on pasta salad, or a fruited green salad with slices of fresh plums, mixed greens and toasted nuts.

Mermaids of Mark Island – 1966

Vegetables

Grilled Vegetables

Roasted Asparagus with
  Balsamic Browned Butter

Broccoli Casserole

Fresh Corn Pudding

Lime Corn-on-the-Cob

Summer Squash Casserole

Fried Zucchini Sticks

Potatoes

Garlicky Baby Potatoes

Campfire Potato Wedges

Grilled Cheese Potatoes

Island Potato Fans

Lockes Island
  Potato Challenge

Marinated Grilled
  Sweet Potatoes

Sweet Potato Casserole

Grains and Beans

Armenian Rice Pilaf

Black Beans and Rice

Traditional Baked Beans

Easy Baked Beans

Baked Pasta

Welch Island
  Spinach Lasagna

Meat Lasagna

Tossed Pasta

Summertime Pasta

Chicken Pepper Pasta

Pasta Sauces

Fresh Tomato Pasta Sauce

Pesto Sauce

Browned Butter
  and Herb Sauce

Grilled Vegetables

Kathleen Aceto ❋ Welch Island

Cut up vegetables: peppers, eggplant, zucchini, yellow squash, asparagus, purple onions and fennel. Place in a large plastic bag. Sprinkle with olive oil (enough to coat veggies), salt pepper, and a tablespoon of whatever fresh herbs you have (basil, parsley, oregano, chives...) Place on warm grill, cooking until just soft, turning once. Arrange on large platter and sprinkle with balsamic vinegar. Crumbled blue cheese or feta cheese can also be sprinkled on top.

Roasted Asparagus with Balsamic Browned Butter

Daryl Thompson ❋ Welch Island

Credit goes to Brenda McGee for this delicious recipe.

2 pounds fresh asparagus spears, cleaned and trimmed
¼ teaspoon kosher salt
⅛ teaspoon pepper
2 tablespoons butter
2 teaspoons soy sauce
1 teaspoon balsamic vinegar

Preheat oven to 400°F.

Arrange asparagus in a single layer on a baking sheet.
Sprinkle with olive oil and season with salt and pepper.
Bake 15 – 20 minutes.

While asparagus is baking, melt butter in a small skillet over medium heat. Heat 3 minutes or until lightly browned, swirling pan occasionally, being careful not to let the butter burn.

Remove skillet from heat. Stir in soy sauce and vinegar.
Drizzle sauce over asparagus, tossing to coat.
Serve immediately.

❋ ❋ ❋ ❋ ❋

LIFE EXPECTANCY WOULD GROW BY LEAPS AND BOUNDS IF GREEN VEGETABLES SMELLED AS GOOD AS BACON. Doug Larson

Broccoli Casserole

Mary Dexter ✳ Welch Island

2 tablespoons butter
2 tablespoons flour
3-ounces cream cheese
¼ cup crumbled blue cheese
1 cup milk
2 (10-ounce) packages frozen chopped broccoli
Cracker crumbs

Preheat oven to 350°F. Butter an 8 x 12-inch baking dish.
Melt butter in a large pot. Blend in flour and cook for 1 minute.
Whisk in milk and cheeses.
Cook, stirring until mixture boils. Stir in broccoli.
Turn broccoli mixture into baking dish.
Top with cracker crumbs. Bake for 30 minutes.

Fresh Corn Pudding

Jeannette Buell ✳ Mark Island

From the Blueberry Hill Cookbook by Elsie Masterton.
You will love this! You may never eat corn "on the cob" again.

12 to 15 large ears of corn
1 tablespoon sugar
1 tablespoon flour
1 teaspoon salt
½ cup melted butter
1 cup light cream

Preheat oven to 350°F. Butter a 2-quart baking dish.
Cut and scrape kernels from the ears of corn – you should have a quart.
If necessary, scrape a few more ears to make a full quart.
In a large bowl, blend together sugar, flour and salt. Add corn kernels and toss until well coated. Pour melted butter and cream over corn and stir until combined. Pour corn mixture into the prepared pan. Bake pudding for 1 hour or until the pudding is golden and bubbly. Be careful not to over-bake.

Apparently, the cats got wind of the event, and a couple of them disappeared for the day. Fortunately, we were able to draft a couple of pet rabbits as last minute substitutes, this being that they either liked the water better than cats, or were dumber.

A large number of craft were entered in the competition. One of the more seaworthy vessels was a Styrofoam cooler with hollowed-out half zucchinis for outriggers. Another was designed after the Kon-Tiki raft with hollow zucchinis stuffed with Styrofoam, and equipped with a sail. Another, the designer more aware of cat aversion to water, came equipped with a wire cage to discourage pre-mature abandoning of ship. One contestant submitted a dead bat stapled to a cedar shingle. When questioned about the design, the response was, "Oh, I thought you said "Bat/zini!"

The animals survived their ordeal. In fact the rabbits seemed to enjoy all the attention, and took to the water like golden retrievers. (You guessed it, not all craft were seaworthy enough.) Prizes were awarded, everyone had a great time, and we were able to deplete our supply of zucchinis without having to eat them all.

Cat/zini Aqua Sail   Photo Courtesy of Ray Keating

Fried Zucchini Sticks

Ray Keating ❋ Mark Island

If you can't find a way to rid yourself of gift zucchinis, here's a recipe that makes them easy to swallow.

Untold quantities of zucchini
1 cup milk
1 cup flour
Salt and pepper
1 or 2 eggs beaten
1 or 2 tablespoons milk
1 cup plain bread crumbs
1 quart vegetable oil

Any number of dipping sauces

Peel zucchini then slice lengthwise in ½ inch slabs.
Lay slabs flat; slice across into ½ inch sticks (like French fries).
Soak zucchini sticks in milk for a couple of minutes.
Season the flour with salt and pepper.

Beat eggs with the addition of 1 tablespoon of milk per egg.
Drain milk from zucchini; dredge in seasoned flour.

Dip floured sticks into egg mixture, shake of excess then roll in bread crumbs.
Place breaded sticks on a rack and allow to set-up for at least 20 minutes.

Heat frying oil to 375°F. Fry zucchini sticks, a few at a time until golden brown. Drain on paper towels or paper bags; serve while hot. Choose your favorite dipping sauce.

Suggested Dipping sauces:
Marinara
Horseradish
Gingered-Soy
Any cream-based salad dressing

Garlicky Baby Potatoes

Jenni Gemberling ✳ Barndoor Island

Adjust the amount of potatoes to the number of your guests.
Cook extra – they make for tasty home fries in the morning.

1 5-pound bag new potatoes, red, gold or a combination
Olive oil
Garlic
Salt & pepper

Spread cleaned potatoes on a baking sheet. Coat with olive oil, sprinkle with salt, pepper and garlic.

Bake at 400°F. for 45 minutes to one hour or cook wrapped in foil on the grill.

Campfire Potato Wedges

Joanne and Tim Moulton ✳ Sleepers Island

Potatoes (one per person)
Cheese
Bacon, cooked and crumbled
Herbs

Quarter the potatoes. Cover with cheese, cooked bacon, and herbs.
Wrap in foil and throw on the fire – cook until done!

Note: Un-wrap your foil packets carefully… the trapped steam can burn you!

Catching Some Wake

Grilled Cheese Potatoes

Jan Maynard ❄ Locke's Island

Potatoes, peeled and thickly sliced
Garlic powder
Seasoned salt
Paprika
Grated Parmesan cheese
Butter

Spray a large sheet of foil (or two sheets of foil, depending on the number of people to be served) with cooking spray. Lay potatoes in overlapping rows on foil. Sprinkle heavily with seasonings and cheese; dot with butter. Seal foil around potatoes. Grill for 25–30 minutes, turning once.
As an alternative to the grill, place foil package on a cookie sheet and bake in the oven at 425°F. for 30–35 minutes.

Note: *Benecol* works well as a substitute for the butter in this.

Island Potato Fans

Anne Bean ❄ Little Camp Island

One potato per person, scrubbed
Yellow onion, sliced
Butter
Salt
Pepper

Being careful not to cut all the way through, make slices across the full length of each potato, ¼" to ½" apart.
Gently part the cuts and insert a slice of onion and pat of butter in each. Make individual packets by placing a stuffed potato on foil, season with salt and pepper and seal.
Arrange on a preheated grill and cook for 30– 45 minutes depending on the size of potatoes and temperature of grill. Unwrap and eat.

Lockes Island Potato Challenge

Priscilla Mayo Sutcliffe ❋ Lockes Island

Chunks or slices? This debate started several years ago when two men, Peter Sutcliffe and Roger Tropf, along with their wives, shared grills and dinners at each other's camps. We met our friends the Tropf's in 1989 when they bought their camp on Lockes Island. We connected instantly and today consider them the family we picked!

Peter's version:
4 medium red potatoes, skin on, cut into chunks
2-4 cloves garlic minced or garlic powder
Minced onion or onion powder
¼ cup or more olive oil
Italian seasoning or any seasonings you have on hand
Pepper and sea salt to taste

Toss potato chunks, garlic and onion with oil and seasonings in an oven-proof dish or skillet with a cover. Let marinate for a while.

Preheat the grill to medium. Place covered dish or skillet on the grill for half-hour, tossing a few times, until potatoes are just tender.

Roger's version:
Olive oil
Yukon Gold or Russet potatoes, sliced thin
Garlic
Salt and pepper
1 large Vidalia onion, sliced thin

Coat a baking dish that can be placed on the grill with olive oil.
Layer potatoes, garlic, salt, pepper and onions in pan. Drizzle with oil.
Repeat this layering and top with more olive oil.

Cook in covered dish on hot grill for 20-25 minutes.

Chunked versus sliced… you decide.

Marinated Grilled Sweet Potatoes

Muriel Robinette ❊ Cow Island

These are so liked by our family and friends that I plan on 1 potato per person, even if the potatoes are huge.

The marinade recipe can be flexible depending on what you have available on the island. My family likes them pretty tangy so I tend to go heavy on the spices. Just be sure to follow the general rule of a marinade, in that your substitutions include something oily (vector for the flavors), something sour (helps break down the flesh for marinade penetration) and something sweet (helps balance the sour).

4-6 large sweet potatoes, scrubbed, unpeeled, cut into ¾ inch slices

⅔ cup oil
½ cup rice vinegar
¼ cup *A-1* sauce
½ cup maple syrup
3 cloves garlic, chopped (or ½ teaspoon garlic powder)
1 teaspoon salt (or soy sauce)
Freshly ground pepper

½ cup chopped, fresh parsley

In a large pot, bring sliced sweet potatoes to a boil; reduce heat to medium-high, cooking for 5 minutes. The potatoes should still be very firm.
Pour off hot water and cool quickly in an ice bath.

In a large bowl, combine oil, vinegar, *A-1* sauce, maple syrup, garlic, salt, pepper and parsley. Toss in cooled potato slices.

Marinate at room temperature for 3 hours or more.
Drain off marinade, reserving for basting.

Place potato slices in a grilling basket; sear over an open fire, pre-heated grill, or under the broiler, turning once during cooking time.

Brush with additional marinade until crisp on the outside.

Sweet Potato Casserole

Evy Chapman ❊ Chase Island

I had sweet potatoes, but not enough of the other ingredients I needed for a recipe. Not wanting to go ashore, I went on-line, found several recipes, combined them, and came up with this recipe that's now my family's favorite.

5 large sweet potatoes
4 ounces cream cheese, softened
1 tablespoon brown sugar
1 teaspoon cinnamon
¼ teaspoon nutmeg

Topping:
½ cup brown sugar
2 tablespoons flour
¼ cup butter, cubed
½ cup crunchy cereal, crushed
⅔ cup pecans, chopped

Microwave sweet potatoes, turning occasionally, 15-18 minutes or until soft. Cut in half; cool for 15 minutes.

Preheat the oven to 350°F. Butter a 7x11-inch baking pan.

Scoop the flesh of the potato out of skins and place in a mixing bowl.
To the bowl, add cream cheese, brown sugar, cinnamon and nutmeg.
Mix until thoroughly combined.
Transfer potato mixture to the prepared baking dish.

For the topping:
In a small bowl, combine brown sugar, flour and butter.
Using a pastry blender, cut ingredients together until the mixture resembles a coarse crumble.
Stir in cereal and pecans.

Sprinkle topping over potato mixture.
Bake for 30 minutes or until heated through.

Armenian Rice Pilaf

Helen Denley ❋ Welch Island

I have served Mrs. Movsessian's recipe for rice at the camp on Welch Island hundreds of times, as it serves a crowd. It's easy to prepare and is always good.

4 tablespoons butter
½ cup vermicelli, broken
1½ cups *Uncle Ben's* long grain rice, (do not use instant)
1 tablespoon salt, scant
2 cups chicken broth
2 cups water

Sauté vermicelli in butter until pink, not brown.
Add rice and salt; stir to coat with butter.
Add broth and water; cook over low to medium heat until liquid is absorbed – stirring often with a wooden spoon…yes, a wooden spoon!

THE DIGGINS
Welch Island - Gordon & Helen Denley
Our camp "Denley's Diggins" was built in 1958. It's now over 50 years old and we are working on 4 generations of memories galore.

Black Beans and Rice

Sean and Wendy Hanley ❋ Welch Island

Adjust the amount of rice and water to the number of people you are feeding. Cook rice according to package directions.

Rice
Water or stock
1 tablespoon butter
1~2 teaspoons cumin, added to rice when cooking.

Add to rice before serving:
1 (15-ounce) can black beans, drained, rinsed with hot water to warm them.
Garnish with fresh parsley or cilantro for color.

Traditional Baked Beans

Nancy L. Buell ❄ Mark Island

These beans were made at home and carried to the island for our hot dog cookouts.

1 pounds beans, cleaned and soaked overnight
1 onion, peeled and halved
½ cup molasses
¼ cup brown sugar
2 teaspoons dry mustard
½ teaspoon pepper
1 teaspoons salt
2 cups boiling water
½ pound salt pork, scored

After the beans have soaked overnight, bring them to a boil, reduce heat and parboil until the skins have cracked.
Drain and pour into a bean pot for baking.
Nestle the onion halves down into the beans.
In a small bowl, combine molasses, brown sugar, dry mustard, pepper and salt with the boiling water. Pour seasoning liquid over the beans. If beans are not completely covered by liquid, add more boiling water to cover.
Place scored salt pork on top and cover bean pot with lid.
Bake at 300°F. for 6-8 hours. Uncover the last ½ hour of baking time.

Easy Baked Beans

Karen Dean ❄ Lockes Island

6 (16-ounce) cans *Campbell's* Pork & Beans
1 pound bacon, cooked crisp, crumbled
1 onion, chopped
3 tablespoons ketchup
1 tablespoon *Grey Poupon* mustard
½ cup brown sugar

Combine all ingredients in a crockery cooker. Cook for a minimum of 4 hours - but the longer you simmer, the better they are.

Note: We liked this with caramelized onions too.

Welch Island Spinach Lasagna

Carole and Bob Jones ❄ Welch Island

Artichoke hearts or mushrooms make a nice addition to this.

10 whole wheat lasagna noodles, uncooked
16 ounces fresh baby spinach
2-3 large tomatoes, sliced ¼ inch thick
Several fresh basil leaves, sliced
1 package sliced provolone
2 (16-ounce) jars *Classico* 4-cheese Alfredo sauce
¼ teaspoon red pepper flakes
¼ cup white wine or vegetable stock
½ cup Parmesan cheese

Preheat oven to 375°F.
Butter or oil a deep 13x9-inch baking dish.

In the bottom of the prepared baking dish, begin layering ½ of these ingredients in the following order:
Lasagna noodles, spinach, sliced tomatoes, basil leaves, provolone cheese.

Top with 1 jar of Alfredo sauce, and then repeat layering. After you have completed the layers, finish with the second jar of Alfredo sauce.

Drizzle with white wine, and then sprinkle the top with red pepper flakes and Parmesan cheese.

Cover with aluminum foil.
Bake for 45-50 minutes, removing foil for the last 10 minutes.

Remove from oven; let rest for 10 minutes before cutting.
Serve with crusty bread and a cold, crisp salad.

Billy Buell Watches Harry Bryant Clear the View on Mark Island

Meat Lasagna

Mary Dexter ❋ Welch Island

1 pound lean ground beef
1 medium onion, chopped
1 clove garlic, minced
1½ teaspoon oregano
1 teaspoon basil
1 teaspoon salt
¼ teaspoon pepper
2 (6-ounce) cans tomato paste
2 cups hot water
1 (8-ounce) package lasagna noodles
1 (16-ounce) container ricotta cheese
8-ounces mozzarella, sliced
½ cup grated Parmesan

In a large skillet, brown beef with onion and garlic.
Drain off fat.
Add oregano, basil, salt, pepper, tomato paste and water to pan.
Simmer uncovered for 30 minutes.

Meanwhile, cook lasagna noodles according to package directions.

Spoon a thin layer of sauce into a 13x9-inch baking dish. Cover with half the cooked noodles.
Spread with half the ricotta and half the mozzarella slices.
Carefully spread half the remaining meat sauce over mozzarella.
Cover with the rest of the noodles, ricotta and mozzarella cheeses.
Top with the remaining sauce and sprinkle with Parmesan cheese.

Bake at 350 F. for 40-45 minutes.
Let stand 10 minutes before cutting.

❋ ❋ ❋ ❋ ❋

TO SUCCEED IN LIFE, YOU NEED THREE THINGS: A WISH BONE, A BACKBONE AND A FUNNY BONE. Reba McEntire

Summertime Pasta

Nancy McNitt ❄ Spider Island

This is one of my favorite summertime dishes. Everyone loves it!
So easy and good with just about everything.

4 medium ripe tomatoes, coarsely chopped
4 cloves garlic, minced
½ cup fresh basil chopped or dried basil to taste
2 teaspoons salt
½ teaspoon freshly ground black pepper
¼ teaspoon hot pepper flakes
½ cup olive oil

3 boneless chicken breasts, basted with either barbecue sauce, or salad dressing
1 pound small macaroni shells
½ cup freshly grated Parmesan cheese
½ pound Fontina cheese, finely diced

In a medium bowl, toss together the tomatoes, garlic, basil, salt, pepper, hot pepper flakes and olive oil.

Let stand at room temperature for 3 hours, stirring occasionally.

Grill basted chicken until cooked through. Cool then cut into bite size pieces.

Cook the pasta in a large pot of boiling salted water, until al-dente.
Drain. Transfer to a serving bowl.

Spoon ¼ cup of liquid from the tomato mixture and toss with the cooked pasta. While the pasta is still hot, add the Parmesan and Fontina cheeses; toss until the cheeses begin to melt.
Add the tomatoes and their liquid; toss until mixed.
Toss in chicken.

Serve warm or at room temperature.

We purchased our 9 Mark Island land approximately 54 years ago—best thing we have ever done!

Our children, David and Dale Anne, grew up at this beautiful place and now their families are Mark Islanders, too.

We didn't bother with electricity for many years, but did become civilized, sort of, when we hooked up. Rusty built our screen house about 15 years ago. We gave up the cooler and the old camping stove at that time and installed a small refrigerator and little stove for cooking. We later purchased a small cast-iron stove to keep us warm and Rusty fitted the porch with see-through, removable, plastic panels from a florist's greenhouse supplier. These are stored in an outside rack until we need them on stormy days.

We know we have arrived when the canning jar, filled with wild flowers, is placed on the table along side a pair of old wooden ducks.

We all sleep in tents and guests set up their own tents as well, and the calls of the loons 'lullaby' us to sleep. We look like gophers as we come out at daybreak!

We have wonderful neighbors and millions of dollars worth of memories. Magical!

Browned Butter and Herb Sauce

Jeannette Buell ✳ Mark Island

Make the perfect side dish for whatever meat you are serving by swapping out the herbs, bouillon or cheese.

½ cup unsalted butter
1 bouillon cube - beef, chicken or vegetable
2 sprigs of either sage or rosemary
2 tablespoons finely grated Parmesan or Romano cheese
Freshly ground black pepper or red pepper flakes, to taste
1 pound cooked pasta, any shape

Watching carefully, brown the butter in a large sauce pan with bouillon and herb sprigs. Remove pan from the heat when you have achieved the desired color. Remove the herb sprigs from sauce then stir in the cheese and pepper. Toss the sauce into steaming hot pasta. Top with additional grated cheese.

Harold and Daryl Dexter Displaying "The Catch of the Day"

Fish

Hal's Broiled Lake Trout

Adriatic Fish Bake

Flounder with Lemon Butter

Baked Stuffed Haddock

Tilapia in Lemon Caper Sauce

Grilled Swordfish Steaks

Welch Island Fish and Veggie Fry

Sunfish-Catching Dough Balls

Ginger Salmon

Salmon Steak with Mango Salsa

Glazed Asian Salmon

Salmon with Mushrooms
and Tarragon Cream

Shellfish

Crab Legs with Tequila-Citrus Butter

Lime Cilantro Shrimp with Mango Salsa

Spicy Grilled or Broiled Shrimp

Elegant Scallops

Scallops Sauté Meunière

Lobster Thermidor

Hal's Broiled Lake Trout with Pernod

Harold C. Lyon ❄ Bear Island

Hal Lyon is the author of "Angling In the Smile of the Great Spirit: Six Centuries of Wisdom from the Master Anglers of Lake Winnipesaukee." Thank you, Hal. We can't imagine a better source for the perfect lake trout recipe.

2 fresh caught lake trout fillets (2-4 pound fish)
Olive oil
Salt
1 cup *Cornflake* crumbs
½ fresh lemon, cut into 2 wedges
1 tablespoon fresh chopped basil, divided
2 teaspoons fresh chopped dill, divided
1 tablespoon *Pernod*
½ cup grated sharp Cheddar cheese
½ cup sliced almonds

Preheat broiler for at least 3 minutes. Adjust your oven rack to second rung from top. Line a baking sheet with aluminum foil.
Brush the flesh side of fillets with olive oil, sprinkle with a little salt and coat in cornflake crumbs. Place fillets, skin-side down on prepared baking sheet. Sprinkle fillets with the juice of one lemon wedge, half of the basil and half of the dill. Drizzle with *Pernod*.
Broil fillets for 5 minutes. Remove from oven; turn fillets over.
Brush skin side with olive oil, cover with cornflake crumbs, and sprinkle with juice from remaining lemon wedge. Sprinkle with the rest of the basil and dill. Cover with grated cheese.
Broil an additional 5 minutes.

Remove from oven and sprinkle with sliced almonds.
Place back under hot broiler for 1 more minute or until almonds are browned and cheese is melted, being careful not to over cook.

Options: This recipe can also be done on a grill with fillets wrapped in foil, but again, be careful not to overcook.

Serve with polenta or grits and a salad.

Also try baking a (4-5 pound) lake trout:
Stuff with easy to prepare *Pepperidge Farm Stuffing,* otherwise using the same ingredients. Bake for 30 minutes at 375°F.
Take it out, top with cheese, almonds and *Pernod* and then bake a final 5 minutes until the cheese melts.

See a demonstration of Hal cooking Lake trout on the Island in his DVD, "A Love Affair with Angling – Disc 2," available at underlineunderline deepwaterspress.com.

Adriatic Fish Bake

Renate and Dick Marcoux ❋ Mark Island

1 leek, white part only, sliced into rings
1 large sweet onion, diced
½ cup chopped celery
½ cup shredded carrots
1 green pepper, seeded, sliced
1 yellow pepper, seeded, sliced
3-5 tomatoes, diced
1 bunch of parsley, minced
8 slices lean smoked bacon
2 pounds skinless white fish fillets
Salt and pepper
1 cup heavy cream
1 cup sour cream
2 tablespoons cornstarch

Preheat oven to 350°F. Butter a 13x9-inch baking dish.
Place leek, onion, celery, carrots, peppers, tomatoes and ½ the parsley in the bottom of prepared baking dish.
Arrange 4 slices of bacon on top of vegetables.
Salt and pepper the fish; lay on top of bacon.
Top the fish with the remaining 4 slices of bacon.
Depending on the thickness of fish fillets, bake for 15-30 minutes or until vegetables and fish are nearly cooked.
Mix together heavy cream, sour cream and cornstarch; pour over fish.
Return to oven and continue to bake for another 10-15 minutes. Garnish with remaining parsley.

Racing in the Rain

Flounder with Lemon Butter

Louise McKean ❈ Mark Island

This reverse egg wash method is perfect for any white fish. Try it on chicken cutlets too.

1 small package slivered almonds
½ cup butter, divided
¾ cup flour
1 teaspoon seasoned salt (such as *Morton Nature's Season*)
2 eggs, beaten
1 pound flounder
2 lemons juiced
Italian parsley to garnish

Preheat oven to 300°F.

Sauté the almonds in 1 tablespoon of butter, watching carefully so that they don't burn. Remove from pan and set aside.
Combine flour and seasoning in a large shallow dish. In a second shallow dish, beat the eggs.

Melt 3 tablespoons of butter in a non-stick pan.
Coat each piece of fish with the seasoned flour, then dip the fish into the egg.
Sauté coated fish for 4-5 minutes, turning once.
Place cooked fish on an oven safe serving platter; keep warm in the oven while you make the sauce.

Melt the remaining 4 tablespoons of butter in pan. Add lemon juice and reduce by bringing sauce to a boil then simmering for 2-3 minutes.
Sprinkle almonds on fillets then pour the sauce over the top.
Garnish with parsley.

Baked Stuffed Haddock

Daryl Thompson ❈ Welch Island

Buy about ½ pound of fish per person. Sprinkle the fish with lemon juice and top it with the seafood stuffing mixture from the fish deli department, or with crushed *Ritz* crackers mixed with melted butter.

Bake at 400°F. for 15-20 minutes, depending on the thickness of the fish.

Tilapia in Lemon Caper Sauce

Mary Dexter ❋ Welch Island

4 (6-ounce) Tilapia fillets, lightly floured
3 tablespoons vegetable or canola oil
2 tablespoons diced onions
4 tablespoons butter
1½ tablespoons capers, drained
½ cup white wine
¼ cup lemon juice
Salt and pepper to taste
Finely chopped parsley

Heat oil in a large sauté pan over high heat.
Place lightly floured Tilapia fillets in pan.
Sear fish on one side until golden brown, turning after 3-4 minutes.
Add onions to the pan - when they're transparent, add butter, capers, white wine and lemon juice. Season with salt and pepper.
Reduce heat to medium and simmer - no longer than 5 minutes.
When sauce becomes silky, add parsley.

Grilled Swordfish Steaks

Daryl Thompson ❋ Welch Island

4 (1-inch thick) swordfish steaks
¼ cup mayonnaise
1 lemon, freshly squeezed for juice
¼ cup butter, melted
Salt
Black pepper
Parsley, chopped (for garnish)

Heat grill to high heat.
Rinse swordfish steaks in cold water and pat dry.
Spread the mayonnaise generously on bottom of swordfish steaks and place on grill. Spread mayonnaise on the top side.
Grill about 6 minutes on each side, depending on thickness of steaks.
Fish is done when it flakes easily with a fork.
Add the lemon juice to the melted butter and serve on the side.
Sprinkle steaks with salt and pepper and serve hot on a serving platter, garnished with parsley.

Welch Island Fish and Veggie Fry

Bob and Carol Jones ✳ Welch Island

I serve this often (well, as long as the supply of fish is 'kept up!')
The fish caught off Doc Dexter's place are the sweetest!

Deep fryer
Vegetable oil

Batter:
1 cup all-purpose flour
½ cup corn meal
1 teaspoon baking powder
1-1½ cups beer

Marinade:
Italian style dressing

Zucchini, cut in half and then into 2 x ½-inch sticks
Artichoke hearts, quartered
Mushrooms, halved
Peppers, sliced into strips
Etc…

Fillets of bass and perch, halved (serving size)

Sea salt
Grated Parmesan cheese

Fill the deep fryer with vegetable oil and heat to *fish-frying* temperature (350°F.-375°F.).

Batter: In a bowl, mix together flour, cornmeal, baking powder and enough beer to create a batter that is the consistency of a thin crepe batter.

Shake excess dressing from vegetables; dip in the batter and fry until golden brown. Drain on brown paper or paper towels and season with salt and grated Parmesan cheese.

Marinate the fish in the dressing for no more than 10 minutes, so as to enhance rather than overwhelm the flavor of the fish. Dip fish fillets in batter and fry until golden and cooked through.
Drain on paper and season with sea salt.

ICE FISHING
Lockes Island – Nelson Maynard

A story recounted to me by my father, John Maynard, dates back to the early 1920's. To go ice fishing in the winter they would take the train from Concord to Lakeport and then find an alternate way to Glendale, since the train along the lakeshore did not operate in the winter.

One weekend my father and his friends arrived in a snow storm. The roads were not plowed, so they decided to follow the railroad track and walk the nearly five miles in deep snow to Glendale, from where they would cross the ice to Lockes Island. Of course this meant carrying provisions, clothes, etc... It was a long and grueling hike and after passing through Glendale at dusk they staggered on to camp on the east side of Lockes and settled in for the night.

Early the next morning they had a visitor – Frank Bates, who lived at Glendale and ran the store. He told Dad that he saw them pass by the previous night and figured that they had to be "damn drunk or damn tired" and that he just had to find out which. Fishing was good. Some people will do anything to go fishing!

"I Have Worms."
Frank Bates in Glendale in the Early 1920s
Photo Courtesy of Nelson Maynard

Salmon with Mushrooms and Tarragon Cream

Kitty Leonardson  Welch Island

¼ cup unsalted butter
¾ pound fresh mushrooms, thinly sliced
2 cups dry white wine or dry vermouth
4 salmon fillets (5-6 ounces each)
2 tablespoons chopped fresh tarragon
1 cup heavy cream
Salt
Freshly ground pepper

In a larger skillet over medium heat, melt butter.
Add mushrooms, sautéing 3-5 minutes, just until tender.
Remove mushrooms and juices from skillet; set aside.

Deglaze pan by pouring white wine into pan and bringing it to a boil over high heat, scraping any bits adhered to the bottom with a spatula.

Reduce heat to medium-low. Add salmon to pan and cover.
Poach salmon until opaque, about 8 minutes.
Using a slotted spoon, transfer salmon to a warm serving platter - cover with plastic wrap and keep warm.

Raise heat to high, reducing pan juices to a glaze.
Stir in mushrooms, tarragon and cream - season with salt and pepper to taste.
Cook 1-2 minutes longer.
Spoon the mushroom sauce over the salmon fillets.
Serve immediately.

※ ※ ※ ※ ※

What's swimming with you in Lake Winnipesaukee?

There are salmon, rainbow trout, brook trout, lake trout, small-mouth bass, large-mouth bass, pickerel, hornpout, yellow perch, white perch, cusk, smelt, and white fish, plus turtles--and the occasional eel.

Crab Legs with Tequila-Citrus Butter

Christine Keating ❋ Mark Island

1 cup butter
½ cup fresh lime juice
¼ cup tequila

3 quarts water
1 tablespoon *Old Bay Seasoning*
12 Alaskan king crab legs, shells cut lengthwise

2 limes cut into wedges

Melt butter with lime juice in medium sauce pan over medium-low heat.
Let simmer 4 minutes. Remove from heat and add tequila.
Return pan to medium-low heat; whisk until butter begins to simmer.
Keep warm.

Bring 3 quarts of water and *Old Bay Seasoning* to a boil in a large, heavy roasting pan, set over 2 burners.
Add crab legs. Cover pan tightly with foil.
Cook just until heated through – about 4 minutes.

Divide the crab among 6 plates.
Pour flavored butter into 6 ramekins.
Serve crab with tequila-citrus butter.
Garnish with lime wedges.

Travis Shute and Emily Parker with their Catch

Lime Cilantro Shrimp with Mango Salsa

Wendy and Sean Hanley ✳ Welch Island

This marinade is also great on swordfish and chicken.

2 pounds extra-jumbo shrimp

Lime Cilantro marinade:
3 cloves garlic
1 cup packed fresh cilantro
2 teaspoons grated lime zest
½ cup lime juice
½ cup olive oil
1 teaspoon salt
½ teaspoon pepper

Blend together all marinade ingredients in a blender or processor.
Combine the shrimp with the marinade: Allow to marinate for 2-4 hours.
Thread shrimp onto skewers. Grill until cooked through.

Serve on black beans and rice topped with mango salsa.

Mango Salsa:
2 ripe mangos, diced
1 red pepper, seeded, and diced
1 jalapeno, seeded, and diced
1 avocado, peeled and diced
½ red onion, diced
2 tablespoons lime cilantro marinade

Toss salsa ingredients together.
Store in an air-tight container (keeps 2 days).

Note: If you are not a fan of cilantro, substitute flat-leaf parsley.

✳ ✳ ✳ ✳ ✳

Tip: A microplane grater is perfect for zesting the citrus in this recipe.
Use it for grating garlic and ginger too, in dressings and marinades.

Spicy Grilled or Broiled Shrimp

Daryl Thompson ❋ Welch Island

This is a favorite, originating from our well-traveled friend, Susan Howe.

1½–2 pounds shrimp, (20-30 size), peeled, rinsed and dried
1 large garlic clove, minced
1 teaspoon coarse salt
½ teaspoon cayenne pepper
1 teaspoon paprika
2 tablespoons olive oil
2 teaspoons fresh lemon juice
Lemon wedges

Start a charcoal or gas grill – or preheat the broiler. In any case, make sure the fire is as hot as it will get – or adjust the rack so that it is as close to the heat source as possible.

Mince garlic with salt; mix it with cayenne and paprika, then make it into a paste with olive oil and lemon juice. Smear paste all over shrimp.

Grill or broil shrimp 2-3 minutes per side – turning once.
Serve immediately. Garnish with lemon slices.

Elegant Scallops

Mary Dexter ❋ Welch Island

3 tablespoons butter
½ pound fresh mushrooms, sliced
2 tablespoons flour
1 cup light cream or half-and-half
1 tablespoon dry vermouth
Salt and pepper to taste
1 pound sea scallops, quartered, or whole bay scallops
Ritz cracker crumbs (half a sleeve)
Butter

Heat oven to 375°F.
Lightly butter a small baking dish or individual au-gratin dishes.

In a skillet, melt butter and sauté mushrooms about 5 minutes.
Blend in flour. Add cream slowly, stirring into a thin sauce.
Add vermouth, seasonings, and scallops.

Place in baking dish and top with cracker crumbs.
Dot the top of casserole with butter. Bake 10-15 minutes.

Scallops Sauté Meunière

Ray Keating ❋ Mark Island

Meunière refers to both a sauce and a method of preparation. This is a brown butter sauce with lemon. The method involves dredging with flour and sautéing in butter

3 pounds fresh scallops
1 cup flour
Cooking oil
½ cup butter (1 stick)
1 lemon, divided
2 teaspoons chopped parsley

Wash, drain and dry the scallops on paper towels. Dredge in flour and shake vigorously to remove all excess flour.

In a heavy (preferably cast iron) skillet, pour enough cooking oil to cover bottom ¼-inch of skillet. Heat oil until almost smoking hot.

Cook half the scallops, turning once until both sides are lightly browned, about 5 minutes. Remove with a slotted spoon and drain on paper towels. Keep warm.

Replenish oil again to ¼-inch and repeat cooking with the remaining scallops.

Pour off all fat from the skillet. Add the butter and heat until it turns light brown. Remove skillet from stove at once and add the juice of half the lemon and parsley.

Put browned scallops on a warm platter or in a serving dish. Pour hot butter sauce over them and serve with a garnish of parsley and lemon wedges.

Tips:

To get the most juice out of a lemon (or any citrus fruit), roll fruit on the counter, applying gentle pressure, before cutting it open.
Rub a cut lemon on your fingers to remove fish or garlic odor.

The absence of a center for the performing arts with great acoustical properties does not faze islanders. They often create distinguished musical interludes for the enhancement of their dining experience. Any convenient deck, fireside, or living room can become the site for impromptu musical events.

The Mark Island Brass Ensemble and Buccaneer Band stands by as Maestro Scarponi conducts the audience in a chorus from
The Pirates Of Penzance.

Balladeer Keating presents a soulful rendition of the old mariner's folk song,
Way, Haul Away, We're Stranded on The Witches.
Photos Courtesy of Ray Keating

Lobster Thermidor

Sharon Doyle ❀ Bear Island

This is Kay Sauerbrunn's recipe from the "Deep Cove Party".
This lady knew how to celebrate island life!

Cream Sauce:
3 tablespoons butter
1 teaspoon minced onion
3 tablespoons flour
2 cups milk
½ teaspoon salt
⅛ teaspoon white pepper
1 teaspoon dry mustard
Dash celery salt

1 lobster

4 tablespoons butter
¾ cup sliced mushrooms
Dash paprika
⅛ teaspoon dry mustard
1 tablespoon minced parsley
½ cup sherry
1½ cup cream sauce, divided
2 tablespoons grated Parmesan cheese

Cream Sauce: Melt butter in a sauce pan. Sauté onion until translucent.
Stir in flour and continue to cook for another minute.
Add milk gradually and cook until thickened, stirring constantly.
Add salt, pepper, dry mustard and celery salt.

Preheat oven to 450°F.

Boil and split lobster. Remove meat and cut into small pieces.
Sauté mushrooms five minutes in butter; add paprika, mustard, parsley, sherry
and 1 cup cream sauce.
Stir in lobster pieces.
Fill lobster shells with mixture and cover with remaining cream sauce.
Sprinkle with cheese. Bake for 10 minutes.
Serves 2

Juvenile Eagle Nesting on Round Island

THE CHICKEN COOP
Bear Island – Craig and Renee Richard

We first purchased our house on Bear Island in 1999. Both our kids were in middle school. Two of the bedrooms are in the back of the house. We decided one of them would be ours and the other would be a guest room. The loft upstairs would be where the boys slept.

One of the first times we spent the night, we heard leaves crunching outside. (The deer would come out quite often.) The boys were yelling, "Something's coming!" They came downstairs and wanted to sleep in the spare bedroom. After that we called the room 'the chicken coop" and we've had a wooden sign above that doorway ever since.

Bone-in

Marinated Barbequed Chicken

Easy Barbequed Chicken

Cilantro Chicken with Peach Salsa

Maple Mustard Chicken

Boneless

Parmesan Chicken Breasts

Bacon-Wrapped Chicken Kabobs

Casseroles

Chicken and Bean Cassoulet

Quick Chicken Curry

Chicken and Broccoli Casserole

Chicken and Asparagus Pie

Crunchy Chicken Casserole

Chicken and Bean Cassoulet

Renate Marcoux ❋ Mark Island

Well-seasoned navy beans are complemented with tiny sausage balls and chicken pieces. Accompany this hearty dish with toasted French bread for a very satisfying, crowd-pleasing dinner.

1 pound (2 cups) dry navy beans
8 cups water
1 cup chopped celery
1 cup diced carrot
2 beef bouillon cubes (optional)
1 teaspoon salt
3-4 pound broiler-fryer with giblets, or split boneless breasts
½ pound pork breakfast sausage, links or bulk
Salt
Pepper
Paprika
1 cup chopped onion
1½ cups tomato juice
1 tablespoon Worcestershire Sauce
½ teaspoon paprika

Preheat oven to 325°F.
In a large kettle, combine beans and water.
Bring to a boil and boil for 2 minutes. Remove from heat. Cover.
Let stand for 1 hour. Do not drain.

To beans add celery, carrot, bouillon cubes, salt, neck and giblets from chicken.
Bring to boil, and then reduce heat.
Simmer, covered, for 1 hour.

Shape sausage into small balls and brown in a large skillet. Remove sausage and set aside, reserving drippings.

Season the chicken pieces liberally with salt, pepper and paprika.
Brown in reserved drippings.
Remove chicken; set aside.

In same skillet, cook onion until tender.
Stir in tomato juice and Worcestershire.

Drain bean mixture, reserving liquid. Combine bean mixture, sausage and tomato mixture. Turn into a 6-quart Dutch oven. Top with chicken pieces and pour 1½ cups reserved bean liquid (or tomato juice) over. Cover.
Bake for 1 hour, adding more bean liquid or juice, if needed.

Quick Chicken Curry

Alida Millham ❊ Mark Island

This is a great way to use left over grilled chicken.

1 tablespoon oil
2 cups diced chicken
½ pound thinly sliced mushrooms
⅓ cup chopped onion
3 tablespoons flour
½ teaspoon salt
1 vegetable or chicken bouillon cube
1½ teaspoons curry powder
1 cup chopped apple
¾ cup skim milk
1 cup water

Heat oil in a large skillet.
Sauté chicken, mushrooms and onions, until chicken is browned and onions are soft.
Stir in flour, salt, bouillon and curry powder.
Add apple, milk and water to the skillet.
Bring to a simmer, stirring constantly until sauce is thickened and apples are tender-crisp.
Serve over rice.

Chicken and Broccoli Casserole

Mary Dexter ❊ Welch Island

1 large head fresh broccoli
1 (10.5-ounce) can condensed cream of chicken soup
1 cup mayonnaise
1 teaspoon curry powder
1 teaspoon fresh lemon juice
2-3 boneless chicken breasts, cooked and cubed
1 cup grated Cheddar cheese

Preheat oven to 350°F. Butter a large baking dish.
Cut broccoli into bite-sized pieces and steam to al dente.
Mix together the soup, mayonnaise, curry and lemon juice.
Place broccoli in the bottom of baking dish.
Place cooked chicken on top of broccoli.
Cover with sauce, top with cheese. Bake for 30-40 minutes or until bubbly.

Chicken and Asparagus Pie

Norma Keeler ❋ Bear Island

This may be served as a casserole by exchanging the pie crust for bread crumbs.

1 pound fresh asparagus, cut into 1-inch pieces
3 cups cooked, cubed chicken
6 slices Swiss cheese or sharp Cheddar cheese
2 tablespoons grated Parmesan cheese
1 (10.5-ounce) can condensed cream of chicken soup
¼ cup cooking liquid from asparagus
1 pastry crust or bread crumbs

Preheat oven to 350°F. Butter a 2-quart baking dish.

In a sauce pan, steam asparagus until tender. Reserve ¼ cup cooking liquid when draining.

In the bottom of baking dish, layer half the chicken, half the asparagus, and half the sliced and grated cheeses. Repeat layers.

In a small bowl, dilute soup with reserved cooking liquid.
Pour soup mixture over layers.
Seal the top of baking dish with pie crust or sprinkle with bread crumbs.

Bake for 30-40 minutes or until top is golden brown.

Preparing asparagus:

To remove the tough and stringy end of the stalk, snap-rather than cut- the asparagus and it will break at the right place.
You could also use a vegetable peeler to peel the lower half of the stalk, so as not to waste as much of the asparagus.
To perfectly steam asparagus to al dente, place the prepared stalks in a large skillet with a ¼ inch of water. Do <u>not</u> salt the water, as it dulls the color of the asparagus. Cover the skillet and bring to a boil. As soon as you can smell the asparagus, remove from heat and drain.
Serve immediately, or if serving later - plunge into an ice-bath to stop the cooking process.

Crunchy Chicken Casserole

Rusty and Millie Elwell ❄ Mark Island

Make with leftover chicken or turkey. This can be prepared early in the day, so you can go out and play all day, make a salad and pop the casserole in the oven.

1 tablespoon butter
½ cup chopped onion
1 cup chopped celery
2 cups cubed, cooked chicken
1 (6-ounce) package long grain and wild rice mix, cooked
1 (10.75-ounce) can cream of chicken soup
½ cup sour cream
⅓ cup mayonnaise
1 (5-ounce) can sliced water chestnuts, drained
½ cup sliced almonds
1 teaspoon curry powder
¼ cup parsley, chopped
Salt and pepper to taste

Topping:
½ cup crushed onion-flavored croutons
1 tablespoon melted butter

Preheat oven to 350°F. Butter a 2 ½-quart baking dish.
Melt butter in a large skillet. Sauté onion and celery until tender.
Add chicken, rice, soup, sour cream, mayonnaise, water chestnuts, almonds, curry powder, parsley, salt and pepper.
Stir to combine.
Pour chicken mixture into the prepared baking dish.

Topping: Combine melted butter with the crushed croutons – sprinkle on top of casserole.

Bake for 30 minutes or until heated through.

Tip: To keep your salt shaker free-flowing in humid weather, put a few grains of uncooked dry rice in the shaker.

ISLAND HAPPENINGS
Sleepers Island – Tim and Joanne Moulton

When my daughter, Andrea, was a teenager water skiing around the island, she noticed what she thought was a branch, and yelled, "Drive away!" Then, on second look, she realized it was a deer with a full rack of antlers. Many deer spend the summer on Sleepers.

This year Terri, our oldest daughter, celebrated her special birthday at our island home. Thirty some original neighbors who grew up on the island attended. It was a delightful day.

Special island events consist of simple gatherings of our guests on our dock. We never had a gas grill—we cooked all meals on a wood fire at our dock.

Tip for island living: Don't forget the organization of planning trips to and from the mainland and coordinating trips back. In the early days there were no barges, so many of us pulled supplies over on the ice. We even drove our car over one year. Most of our building materials came over by boat. One time a neighbor was walking on the dock with a roll of carpet and walked right off the end. He was wet, but the carpet was saved. I guess being islanders for 45 years means we all have many tales.

A Gaggle of Canada Geese

LABOR OF LOVE
Lockes Island – Priscilla Mayo Sutcliffe

Islanders all share many unique challenges. Three most frequent are hauling materials and food, maintaining the property, and entertaining guests. The hauling is enough to create a separate book full of wonderful stories. I figure food is handled or transferred a minimum of six times by the time it reaches our mouths. Maintenance never ends and, when we go to close, we often wonder where all our visitors have gone.

Becky's Garden

Beef

Black Angus Beef Tenderloin

Highland Steaks

Filet Mignon with Mustard Caper Sauce

Marinated Steak Tips

Island Grilled Flank Steak

Buffalo Burgers
   with Spicy Mango Ketchup

Cuban Burgers

Stuffed Chipotle Burgers

Enchilada Casserole

Leftover Hamburger Pie

Sleepers Island Beef Supper

Pork

Grilled Pork Rub

Marinated Pork Tenderloins

Apricot Bourbon Chutney

Cranberry Glazed Pork

Lamb

Rack of Lamb with Mustard Crumbs

Braised Lamb Shanks
   with Rosemary and Garlic

Mixed Grill

The Pile

Buffalo Burgers with Spicy Mango Ketchup

Renate Marcoux ❀ Mark Island

1 pound buffalo meat, finely ground
½-1 cup BBQ sauce, (your favorite brand)
Salt and pepper

Divide the meat into four even portions and shape into patties. Brush both sides of each burger with barbecue sauce and season with salt and pepper. Grill for 3-4 minutes on each side.

Mango Ketchup:
2 tablespoons olive oil
1 small onion, chopped
2 cloves garlic, chopped
1 mango, peeled, pitted and chopped
¼ teaspoon allspice
¼ teaspoon ground cinnamon
Pinch of ground cloves
1 habanero pepper, chopped
1 teaspoon honey
½ cup red wine vinegar
Salt
Freshly ground pepper

Heat oil in a medium saucepan over medium-high heat.
Add garlic and onion and cook until soft. Add mango and cook for 5 minutes, until soft. Add cinnamon, allspice, cloves and habanero.
Cook an additional 2 minutes.
Pour mango mixture into a food processor. Add the vinegar and honey. Process the ketchup until smooth.
Season with salt and pepper.
Serve cold or at room temperature.

The Sophie C. - U.S. Mail Boat

Cuban Burgers

Connie Grant ❋ Welch Island

I've been making these for years and we can hardly eat regular burgers now. When we have company, we often do lobster bakes with corn, steamers and potatoes. However, by far, CUBAN BURGERS are the most frequently requested dinner by my company and are a far more economical treat. Bet you can't try them just once!

Roasted Garlic Dijonaise
2 bulbs of garlic, roasted*
¾ cup mayonnaise
¾ cup *Grey Poupon Dijon Mustard*

8 (¼-pound) hamburgers
8 hamburger rolls
8 pieces Swiss cheese
8 (12-inch) squares of foil

Mash the roasted garlic into a paste.
Mix mayonnaise, mustard and roasted garlic together.
Refrigerate sauce until ready to use.

Grill burgers on a preheated grill to medium. Top with cheese and continue to cook, until cheese is melted.

Lay out squares of foil and place one roll bottom on each.
Put a LARGE dollop of roasted garlic dijonaise on each roll.

Put a cooked burger on each bottom and top with the other half of roll. Wrap each burger individually in tin foil.

Place the burgers, tin foil and all, back on the grill and top with a large heavy flat rock. *I found one rock that does all eight burgers at one time but you may want two rocks. What this step does is grills the buns and packs all the delicious flavors together.*

Serve each person a tin foil pouch and let them have the fun of tackling their own burger.

*Recipe for roasted garlic can be found in the appetizer section, page 21.

Chipotle Burgers
Stuffed with Bacon and Cheese

Craig and Renee Richard ※ Bear Island

1 pound ground beef
½ cup shredded Cheddar cheese
6 slices bacon, cooked crisp and crumbled
4 rolls

Chipotle Rub:
3 tablespoons dark brown sugar
1½ teaspoons paprika
½ teaspoon garlic powder
½ teaspoon ground cumin
¼ teaspoon chipotle powder
¼ teaspoon salt
¼ teaspoon pepper

Combine sugar, paprika, garlic powder, cumin, chipotle powder, salt and pepper in a bowl and set aside.
Form the ground beef into 8 equal patties.
Toss the grated cheese and bacon together.
Place equal amounts of cheese mixture on top of 4 beef patties.
Place the remaining patties over the cheese and pinch the edges to seal.
Pat each burger with the spice mixture.
Heat the grill to medium. Grill the burgers about 5 minutes per side.
Serve on rolls with your favorite condiments.

Nancy, Linda, Debbie, Bill and Deems Buell - Hungry at the Grill

Enchilada Casserole

Bobbe Fairman ❈ Camp Island

1½ pounds lean ground beef
1 small onion, chopped
1 garlic clove, minced
1½ cups Picante´ salsa
1 (10-ounce) package frozen chopped spinach, thawed, squeezed dry
1 (8-ounce) can tomato sauce
1 (28-ounce) can chopped tomatoes, un-seasoned
2 medium fresh tomatoes, seeded and chopped
1 large red bell pepper, diced
1 tablespoon lime juice
1½ teaspoons salt
12 corn tortillas
1 cup sour cream
¾ cup shredded Cheddar cheese
¾ cup shredded Monterey Jack cheese
½ cup sliced black olives
Shredded lettuce

Preheat oven to 350°F. Grease a 13x9-inch baking dish.
In a large frying pan, brown meat with onion and garlic; drain.
Add salsa, spinach, tomato sauce, tomatoes, bell pepper, lime juice, and salt.
Simmer uncovered 15 minutes, stirring constantly.

Arrange 6 tortillas on bottom and up sides of prepared baking dish, overlapping
as necessary. Top with half the meat mixture.
Arrange remaining tortillas over first layer.
Spread sour cream evenly over tortillas.
Top with remaining meat mixture.
Refrigerate at this point if making ahead.

Cover with foil. Bake 40 minutes or until hot and bubbly.
Remove from oven; sprinkle with cheeses. Top with sliced olives.

Let stand 10 minutes. Cut into squares and serve.
Garnish with shredded lettuce and additional salsa.
This reheats well.

Leftover Hamburger Pie

Suzanne Morrissey ❋ Bear Island

1 can crescent rolls
1 pound ground beef, or several leftover hamburgers
2-4 slices onion, chopped
Salt and pepper
2 medium tomatoes, sliced thin
5 slices American cheese
3 eggs, separated
¾ cup sour cream
½ cup flour
½ teaspoon salt or salt free seasoning mix
Paprika (optional)

Preheat oven to 350°F.
In an ungreased pie plate, unroll the crescents and press to form a pie crust. Set aside.
In a sauté pan, add beef and onions. Cook until beef is browned and onions are soft. Season with salt and pepper. If using leftover cooked burgers, sauté onion until soft, adding crumbled burger at the end. Heat through.
Drain off any excess fat. Cool.

Transfer cooled beef mixture to prepared pie crust.
Top with sliced tomatoes. Season with salt and pepper. Top with cheese slices.
In a mixing bowl, blend together egg yolks, flour, and sour cream.
Mixture will be lumpy, but that's okay.

In a separate bowl, whisk/beat egg whites into stiff peaks.
Gently fold in egg yolk mixture, until incorporated.
It's okay if it's still lumpy. Spread egg mixture over pie, sealing at edges.
Sprinkle with paprika, if you've got it – if not, more pepper.
Bake 35-40 minutes until topping is puffy and golden brown, and crust is browned. Slice and serve hot.

Special Note: The lower-fat versions of rolls, cheese, and sour cream all work well in this recipe, as does extra-lean ground beef. Add a finely shredded zucchini to get another veggie in there!

Sleepers Island Beef Supper

Susan Brewer ✳ Sleepers Island

1½ pounds ground beef
1 medium onion, peeled and sliced thin
Salt and pepper
3-4 large potatoes, peeled and very thinly sliced
1 cup sour cream
1 (10-ounce) can cream of mushroom soup
1 cup milk
1-2 cups grated Cheddar cheese
Rice Krispies cereal (topping)

Preheat oven to 350°F. Grease a 13x9-inch baking dish.

Brown ground beef and onions in a skillet; season with salt and pepper.
Break beef into small pieces as it cooks; drain off excess fat.
Turn beef mixture into the prepared baking dish.
Arrange potato slices on top of beef.

In a small bowl, mix together sour cream, soup and milk. Pour over potato layer. Sprinkle potatoes with cheese and then with cereal.

Bake 1 hour uncovered or until the potatoes feel fork-tender.
Cut into squares to serve.

Bo Derek
Sizing Up Dinner

Cranberry Glazed Pork

Thelma Malafey ❋ Welch Island

2 pork tenderloins, ¾ pound each
¼ teaspoon salt
¼ teaspoon black pepper

1 cup fresh cranberries
1 cup coarsely chopped peeled apple
⅔ cup packed dark brown sugar
½ cup water
¼ cup chopped onion
1 tablespoon minced, peeled fresh ginger
1 teaspoon curry powder
⅛ teaspoon cayenne pepper

Preheat oven to 350°F. Prepare a broiler pan with cooking spray.
Trim fat and silver skin from pork; season with salt and black pepper.

In a small saucepan, combine cranberries, apple, brown sugar, water, onion, ginger, curry powder and cayenne.
Bring to a boil. Cover, reduce heat, and simmer 20 minutes.
Uncover; simmer 2 minutes or until thick. Cool 10 minutes.

Pour cranberries into a blender or food processor, and process until smooth.
Divide cranberry sauce in half.

Brush pork with half of cranberry sauce. Place pork on broiler pan. Bake for 30 minutes or until thermometer registers 160°F. (slightly pink). Serve pork with remaining cranberry sauce.

Note: If cranberries are out of season, try using blueberries… delicious!

❋ ❋ ❋ ❋ ❋

LIFE IS NOT MEASURED BY THE NUMBER OF BREATHS WE TAKE, BUT BY THE MOMENTS THAT TAKE OUR BREATH AWAY. Unknown

Rack of Lamb with Mustard Crumbs

Walter Johnson ❄ Little Bear Island

If you like lamb, you are going to love this flavor-packed, beautiful dish.

3 thick slices of sourdough bread (for breadcrumbs)
¼ cup plus 2 tablespoons extra-virgin olive oil
¼ cup chopped flat leaf parsley
1½ teaspoons grated lemon zest
5 garlic cloves, 1 minced, 4 unpeeled
Salt and freshly ground pepper
Two 8-inch racks of lamb, Frenched*
2 tablespoons Dijon-style mustard
1½ pounds cherry tomatoes

Preheat oven to 350°F.
Put the bread on a cookie sheet and toast for 10 minutes until golden brown. Let cool, then crumble into pieces. Leave oven on.

Process the toast pieces in a food processor to make crumbs. Transfer crumbs to a bowl and stir in ¼ cup of the olive oil, parsley, lemon zest, and minced garlic. Season with salt and pepper.

In a large skillet, heat 1 tablespoon of the olive oil until shimmering. Season the lamb with salt and pepper. Cook meaty side down over high heat until browned (2 minutes) on both sides. Transfer to a rimmed baking sheet, meaty side up and allow to cool. Spread the mustard over the meaty sides of the racks and then press on the breadcrumb mixture.

Place the tomatoes and 4 unpeeled garlic cloves on another baking sheet and rub with the remaining 1 tablespoon of olive oil. Season with salt and pepper. Put the tomatoes and garlic on the lower rack of the oven and bake for about 25 minutes, until soft.

Meanwhile, put the lamb racks in the center of the oven. Roast the lamb until an instant-read thermometer shows 125°F. (again, about 25 minutes). Transfer lamb to a cutting board and allow to rest for 10 minutes.
Carve lamb into chops and serve with tomatoes and garlic.

❄ ❄ ❄ ❄ ❄

To "French" a bone means to cut the meat away from the end of a rib or chop, so that part of the bone is exposed. This is done with racks of lamb, beef and pork for esthetic reasons. The exposed bones are sometimes covered with frilled papers.

Braised Lamb Shanks
with Rosemary and Garlic

Thelma Malafey ❋ Welch Island

3 tablespoons olive oil
4 whole lamb shanks (approximately 3- 3 ½ pounds)
4-5 cloves garlic, sliced
1 bunch small leeks, sliced crosswise to ½-inch thickness
2 teaspoons chopped fresh rosemary
Salt and pepper
¼ cup dry white wine

In a deep frying pan over medium-high heat, warm oil. When hot but not smoking, add shanks and brown on all sides 10-12 minutes. Transfer to a plate. Reduce heat to medium-low; add garlic and sauté for 30-40 seconds. Add leeks and sauté until translucent, about 6-8 minutes. Return shanks to pan, add rosemary, salt, pepper and wine. Raise heat to medium-high and bring to a simmer. Reduce heat to low, cover and simmer until tender. Turn once or twice during cooking time – about 2-2½ hours. If necessary, add water to maintain original level of liquid.
Season with salt and pepper before serving.

Tyler Buell Waterskiing   Photo Courtesy of Jill Buell

Bridge Connecting Birch and Steamboat Islands

The Pile

Howard and Carol Stoner ❄ Steamboat Island

Howard has perfected "The Pile" over the years. It is always a hit with family and guests.

2 racks of baby back ribs
Pork rib rub
4 large bone-in chicken breasts
8 chicken drumsticks
6-8 *Pale Ale* sausages
KC Masterpiece barbeque sauce

Lightly sprinkle the baby back ribs with the rib rub. Place in a single layer on baking sheets. Cover tightly with foil. Bake at 275°F. for 3 hours

Grill chicken breasts, drumsticks, and sausages for about 45 minutes or until thoroughly cooked.

Turn the grill heat to low.
Form a pile with the meat on the grill and add the cooked ribs to the pile.
Pour barbecue sauce over the meat in the pile.
Let simmer for about 15 minutes.

All of the juices in the meat intermix and add flavor to each other.
Serves 8-10.

WILDLIFE
Sleepers Island - Tim and Joanne Moulton

One year my paper towels in the kitchen were disappearing rapidly. Over the winter a squirrel had eaten a hole in our wall behind the refrigerator. When I was outside the back door, I saw the long piece of toweling hanging down to the ground— the squirrel at the other end!

Four years ago my husband Tim was on his 2-mile hike around the island. He returned quickly, panting, sweating, and out of breath! I asked, "What's wrong?" He said a moose was chasing him. I replied, "Oh, stop. You must have seen a deer." I laughed, and then suddenly I saw the moose peering in our shower window!

Since Tim relayed this story, we have gotten a lot of moose mementos. In 2007, at two different times, we saw moose swimming from the West Alton Marina to our island.

❋ ❋ ❋ ❋ ❋

WILDLIFE ADVENTURE
Treasure Island – Claudette Gammon

We have had interesting wildlife on the island over the years. We have had mink living under one of the boathouses, but we were never able to get photos. The mink were a little too skittish for that.

We've had moose swim from Treasure Island to Rattlesnake, we have had deer drop their antlers when shedding on our lawn, and this year we had wild turkeys living and eating their way around the island.

The most memorable wildlife adventure happened one very hot and steamy night in the early 1980s. We had gone to bed, leaving the door open in the kitchen, with just the screen door shut, to let a cool breeze in from the lake. All of a sudden we heard the screen door start to open-we didn't have a latch on it at the time.

Two raccoons, which we had never had on the island before, thought our garbage can smelled good enough to feast from. There they were, trying to open the screen door, but it kept slamming itself shut.

By then my husband was up and chasing them off. We shut the door. The following weekend we put latches on the screen door!

JoAnn Fagnant-Langan with Great-Grandsons William and Nicholas
Picking and Eating Blueberries

Save your fork for...

Grand Marnier Custard
  with Fresh Blueberries
Berries with Framboise
Strawberry Surprise
Independence Day Fruit Sauce
Red, White & Blueberry Crumble
Chocolate Kahlua Trifle
Éclair Dessert

Cookies

Edith's Snickerdoodles
Gingersnaps
Molasses Cookies
Koulourakia
Fudge Cookies
Easy Peanut Butter Cookies
Congo Bars
Deluxe Butterscotch Brownies
Knighton Family Brownies
Oven S'Mores
Rainy Day S'Mores

Cakes

Rattlesnake Island Blueberry Cake
Grandmother's Blueberry Cake
Blueberry Batter Cake
Sleeper Island Blueberry Cake
Cranberry Cake

Fresh Apple Cake
  with Maple Cream Frosting
Carrot Cake
  with Cream Cheese Frosting
Easy Pineapple Upside-Down Cake
July 4th Anniversary Cake
Kahlua Cake

Pies

Mark Island Pie Crust
Camp Island Pie Crust

Camp Island Blueberry
Barndoor Island Blueberry
Deep Cove Blueberry
Toll House Blueberry
Husband-Stealing Huckleberry
Stonedam Island Deep Dish Apple
No-Crust Swedish Apple
Rhubarb-Orange
Berry Crostada
No-Bake Lemon
Tup's Frozen Key Lime
Key Lime
Crumb Crust
Frozen Chocolate Amaretto
Snickers
4-Minute Brownie

Grand Marnier Custard
with Fresh Blueberries

Marylou Koning ✳ Lockes Island

4 Lockes Island – built by Frank Lougee & S.E. Clark in 1890 – the oldest cottage on the island. My parents, Roy and Mary Cann bought the cottage in September, 1952, and for 56 years it has been enjoyed by three generations. One of the many activities we enjoy during summers at the lake is picking blueberries. The following recipe originally came from the Hickory Stick Farm and is one of our favorite summer treats.

¾ cup sugar
2 tablespoons cornstarch
⅛ teaspoon salt
2 cups milk
4 egg yolks, beaten
2 tablespoons butter
1½ teaspoons vanilla
1½ ounces *Grand Marnier* liqueur
1 cup whipping cream, whipped

3 cups fresh blueberries

In a double boiler, combine sugar, cornstarch and salt, using a whisk to combine. Gradually whisk in milk.
Cook covered over hot water for 8 minutes, without stirring.
Uncover and cook for about 10 minutes more.

In a small mixing bowl, beat the yolks well. Temper the egg yolks by adding a small amount of the hot milk mixture to the yolks, beating in quickly.
Whisk the tempered yolk into the top of double boiler. Add the butter.
Cook and stir these ingredients over hot water for 2 minutes.
Cool to room temperature, stirring occasionally to release steam.

To cooled custard, stir in vanilla and *Grand Marnier.* Fold in whipped cream. Chill.

To serve put a half cup of fresh blueberries in a stemmed glass.
Pour ⅓ cup of *Grand Marnier* custard over berries.

Top with additional whipped cream. Garnish with sprig of mint.
Serves 6.

GOURMET WEEKENDS
Dolly Island – Amelia Welt Katzen

After nearly a decade of renting a tiny island in Tuftonboro, in 1999 we finally found a camp of our own on Dolly Island, just off the southwest tip of Bear Island in Meredith. The primary advantage of having our own place, we discovered, was the ability to invite our friends from home to spend an entire weekend captive on our island. And one of our favorite weekends of the summer has become known among the visitors as the "gourmet" weekend. Four couples come to the island, and everyone loves to eat and cook. Each family is assigned one meal to bring for everyone—and a truly delightful competition seems to have sprung up, resulting in some elaborate and delicious meals.

This brings me to our story. Friday evenings, we always eat late—people inevitably get stuck in traffic, and some arrive at dusk. One Friday evening, as we sat around the dinner table, we were in the middle of the main course when I heard the sound of a screen door slamming. No one else seemed to notice—I looked around the table and counted everyone there. I tried to think who it might have been, but the conversation drew me back and I thought no more about it.

As we were cleaning up after the meal, I went into our back room for a trash bag and noticed a bottle of wine lying in the middle of the floor. There was also a wavy line of white powder, about a foot long, leading to the screen door. I called my friends to see, and Julia exclaimed, "That's the wine I brought." She checked the box of supplies that she'd brought for her meal and said, "Where's my Confectioners' sugar?" She laughed and told us that a small plastic bag of sugar had been in the box under the bottle of wine. It was now clear that a raccoon had rummaged in Julia's box and escaped with his baggie of Confectioners' sugar. He was probably the same sweet-toothed critter that our neighbors had seen eating marshmallows out of the bag next to their barbeque.

Of course, this meant that Julia had to improvise the next night to create her dessert. Luckily the angel food cake was already made, but the frosting she'd planned became a fruit sauce, perfect for the 4th of July, Independence Day Fruit Sauce.

Berries with Framboise

Joanne Dickinson ✳ Mink Island

Credit to Martha Stewart's Quick Cook Menus.

½ pint blackberries
½ pint red raspberries
½ pint blueberries
1 tablespoon Framboise (raspberry liqueur)

Gently toss the berries together in a serving bowl.
Sprinkle with the liqueur and serve. Serves 4

Strawberry Surprise

Margy Knox ✳ Mink Island

1 (3-ounce) package strawberry-flavored *Jell-O*
¾ cup boiling water
1 (10-ounce) package frozen strawberries, partially thawed
1 pint strawberry ice cream
1 angel food cake

Dissolve the *Jell-O* in boiling water.
Add the strawberries and stir until separated.
Add the ice cream and stir until melted.
Tear angel-food cake in pieces and put in 9x9-inch pan.
Pour gelatin mixture over cake and chill until set. Serves 9

Independence Day Fruit Sauce

Amelia Welt Katzen ✳ Dolly Island

Try mashed-up cherries with Cointreau. *If you don't want to use alcohol in your recipe, macerate fresh berries with super fine sugar or a combination of sugar and fruit juice.*

1 cup strawberries cut in quarters
1 cup blueberries
2 teaspoons sugar
2 tablespoons cream sherry (or *Grand Marnier* liqueur)

Mash 6 large strawberries with sugar and cream sherry.
Add cut-up strawberries and blueberries.
Spoon the fruit over slices of angel food cake-or ice-cream.
Sing the Star-Spangled Banner.

Red, White and Blueberry Crumble

Judith Norton ❋ Cow and Pine Islands

5 pints fresh blueberries
2 pints fresh raspberries

10 tablespoons salted butter, softened
1 cup sugar
2 teaspoons vanilla extract
2 teaspoons grated lemon zest
½ cup Confectioners' sugar
2 cups all purpose flour
½ teaspoon salt

Preheat oven to 375°F.
Place the berries in a buttered 11x13-inch glass baking dish.

Cream together softened butter, sugar, vanilla and lemon zest. You can do this by hand or with a mixer. Slowly add Confectioners' sugar, flour and salt.
Mix until combined, being careful not to over work.
Add the topping in clumps, distributing evenly over the top.

Bake for 35 minutes. Serve warm with vanilla-bean ice cream.

Note: if fresh berries are unavailable, 2 (16-ounce) bags of frozen mixed berries, thawed and drained, may be substituted.

❋ ❋ ❋ ❋ ❋

THE WINNI PIT SPIT
Welch Island – Bob and Carol Jones

One summer when my sister was coming from Saratoga Springs, New York, she wondered about all the "welcome race fans" banners. The next trip over she brought a bag of Bing cherries and a "The Winni Pit-Spit" banner that was set up over the front deck of the camp and the "contest" began...

The cherry pits were "spit" from the rail along the porch deck with each "contestant" judged for distance, accuracy and form.

There were comments that some preferred a "clean" pit, others a "fuzzy" pit, etc...
Not necessarily a pretty sight, but there was much cheering, laughing and fun was had by all.

Chocolate Kahlua Trifle

Anne Marie Folsom Ierardi ✳ Round Island

1 (18.25-ounce) box super-moist chocolate cake mix
   Prepare/bake according to package directions.
   (It's best to prepare the cake 24 hours ahead to allow cake to dry.)

1 (5.9-ounce) large box chocolate/dark chocolate instant pudding mix
   Prepare according to package directions. Chill.

1 cup *Kahlua*
1 (8-ounce) container non-dairy whipped topping (*Cool Whip*), thawed
1 package *Heath Bar Crunch* or *Bits of Brickle*
Maraschino cherries, optional

Assemble trifle by dividing ingredients in half and layering in a large trifle or salad bowl.

Cake (cut in cubes)
Kahlua (pour over cake)
Pudding
Cool Whip
Heath Bar Crunch

Repeat layering as above.
Chill for several hours. Top with cherries if desired.

Tip:
Use a vegetable peeler to shave chocolate for garnish. This also works well for shaving hard cheeses.

✳ ✳ ✳ ✳ ✳

LAKE STORE
Rattlesnake Island - Gwen Guilinello

We've had lots of fun living on the "Broads." Big waves, lost in fog and rain at night, and lots of stuff on our breakwater from the lake store. It has been an adventure.

Éclair Dessert

Connie Delaney ❋ Pine Island

Make a day ahead and refrigerate.

Filling:
2 (3-ounce) packages instant vanilla pudding
3 cups milk
1 (8-ounce) carton *Cool Whip*
1 box graham crackers

Icing:
2 packets *Nestles* unsweetened pre-melted chocolate
2 teaspoons light corn syrup
3 tablespoons butter
3 tablespoons milk
1½ cups Confectioners' sugar
1 teaspoon vanilla

Filling:
Blend pudding mix with milk; when pudding has set, fold in the *Cool Whip*.

Butter a 13x9-inch pan.
Arrange ⅓ of the graham crackers in the bottom of pan.
Spread half the pudding mixture on top.
Arrange ⅓ of graham crackers on top of pudding.
Spread with remaining pudding mixture.
Top with remaining graham crackers.

Icing:
In a small mixing bowl blend together icing ingredients until smooth.
Spread icing over all.

Cover and refrigerate overnight. Cut into squares to serve.

Note: If you don't have the Nestles unsweetened pre-melted chocolate, melt unsweetened squares together with the light corn syrup and butter in the top of a double boiler. Be sure to cool before adding the milk, sugar and vanilla.

I'D 'A BAKED A CAKE
Mark Island - Ray Keating

It takes a really special occasion to motivate us to do cakes. One of the first was Chris' father's 60th birthday. For the occasion we took a swimming raft, built a frame on it and covered it with sheets dyed pink. In reference to the annual Winnipesauke Yacht Club Bear Island Stag Cruise, we topped the cake with a rag doll dressed in a bikini. For candles we placed railroad flares at each corner and set them alight. The 'cake' was towed out of hiding in Deep Cove to a prominent position in front of Pascoe's deck.

The cake was a real surprise, especially when the flares burned down and set the pink sheets on fire. The 'cake' burned to the waterline to the delight of all viewers.

"Hey boys, is this Bear Island?"
Photo Courtesy of Ray Keating

Rattlesnake Island Blueberry Cake

Jeannie Leach ※ Rattlesnake Island

This dessert shows up at every Leach family get-together in the summer. It reflects Mary Leach's Eastport, Maine, background, and can feed a crowd. She and Chuck inspired such love for Lake Winnipesaukee in their family that everyone comes back year after year, no matter how far away life takes them. There is no place the three generations would rather be than at the lake.

1½ cups blueberries
2 eggs, separated
1 cup sugar, separated
½ cup butter or margarine, softened
1 teaspoon vanilla
1½ cups flour
1 teaspoon baking powder
¼ teaspoon salt
⅓ cup milk

Preheat oven to 350°F. Grease an 8x8-inch baking pan.

Use a bit of sugar and flour called for in recipe and gently shake into berries. Let stand about ten minutes. This helps to keep them from sinking.

Beat egg whites and ¼ cup of sugar until stiff.
Cream together butter, vanilla and remaining sugar. Gradually add unbeaten egg yolks. Beat till light and creamy.

Sift together flour, baking powder and salt.
Blend dry ingredients into batter, alternately with milk.
Fold in egg whites. Fold in blueberries.

Turn batter into the prepared pan. Sprinkle top of batter lightly with additional sugar.

Bake 350°F. for approximately 50 minutes.

Note: This recipe can be doubled, using a large 9x13-inch pan.

※ ※ ※ ※ ※

RING THE BELLS THAT STILL CAN RING, FORGET YOUR PERFECT OFFERIING. THERE IS A CRACK IN EVERYTHING. THAT'S HOW THE LIGHT GETS IN. Leonard Cohen

Grandmother's Blueberry Cake

Karen McCune ❊ Pine Island

     My family has had our place on Pine Island since 1924 when my grandparents, Helen and Henry Hitt Crane, bought the first two houses. In 1932 they bought the third house along with the boathouse. We have been coming to the lake every year since. I haven't missed a year so far and I am 50.

     When my brothers and I were growing up, we all had meals together in the first house. Grandmother was very punctual with meal times and she'd ring the bell to call us all in. As the blueberries ripened, we'd pick them for Grandmother's blueberry cake. She would serve this at lunchtime. (We have it at any time of the day today!). My second child, Todd, loved this cake so much, it was his birthday cake for years. He even took it to share with his friends at school. This was my wedding cake, decorated by my brothers. We love this simple cake and have passed it around to folks all over the country. Thank goodness our Aunt Jean copied down the recipe for us all, as Grandmother had no recipe, she just made it!

1 stick butter, softened
1 cup sugar
2 eggs
½ cup milk
1 teaspoon vanilla
2 cups flour
1 heaping teaspoon baking powder
1 teaspoon cinnamon
½ teaspoon allspice
½ teaspoon nutmeg
1 heaping cup blueberries

Preheat oven to 350°F. Grease a 9x9-inch baking pan.

In a mixing bowl cream together butter, sugar and eggs; blend in milk and vanilla.

In a separate container combine flour, baking powder and spices. Whisk to distribute.

Stir dry ingredients into batter. Coat the blueberries in a little flour so they will stay evenly distributed in the cake. Fold them into the batter.

Pour batter into the prepared baking pan.
Bake 20-30 minutes. Let cool and enjoy!

Blueberry Batter Cake

Ruth Stewart ❋ Lockes Island

A little history: My grandparents, Roscoe and Edith Suttie built their camp, Timberlight, on Lockes Island in 1938-39. The camp is now owned by Anne Murdock, their daughter, and third-generation grandchildren Bob Whiting and Ruth Stewart, children of Ruth (daughter) and Robert Whiting (both deceased). Edith Suttie died at age 102 in 1993, after spending some part of 43 summers on her beloved island. (There was only one summer during WWII when they did not get there from their home in New Haven, CT). Each summer Gram was the grand hostess for all the children, grandchildren, great-grandchildren and visitors to camp. Her specialties were homemade Root Beer (made when she first arrived) and desserts – especially those made with fresh-picked, New Hampshire wild blueberries! This Blueberry Batter Cake was THE BEST!

2 cups blueberries
1 tablespoon lemon juice

Batter:
1 cup flour
1 teaspoon baking powder
¼ teaspoon salt
¾ cup sugar
3 tablespoons butter, softened
½ cup milk

Topping:
1 cup sugar
1 tablespoon cornstarch
1 cup boiling water

Preheat oven to 375°F. Grease an 8x8-inch baking pan.
Line prepared pan with berries. Sprinkle with lemon juice.

Sift together flour, baking powder and salt.
In a large mixing bowl, cream together sugar and butter.

Alternately, add the dry ingredients and the milk to the creamed butter mixture.
Blend until combined.
Spoon batter evenly over blueberries.

In a small cup, combine the sugar and cornstarch. Sprinkle over batter.
Pour boiling water over all.
Bake for 1 hour.

Sleeper Island Blueberry Cake

Joanne Moulton ❋ Sleeper Island

Island blueberries provide delicious sauces, pancakes, muffins and my favorite…cake.

1½ cups sifted flour
½ teaspoon salt
1 teaspoon baking powder
½ cup butter or margarine
1 cup sugar
2 eggs
1 teaspoon vanilla
1¾ cup blueberries
⅓ cup milk

Preheat oven to 350°F. Grease and flour a 9x9-inch baking pan.

Sift together flour, salt and baking powder.
In a mixing bowl, cream together butter and sugar. Beat in eggs, vanilla and ¼ cup blueberries, mixing until berries are mashed.
Alternating, add sifted dry ingredients and milk to creamed mixture.
Blend to combine.
Stir in the remaining blueberries. Pour batter into pan.
Bake for 35 to 40 minutes.

Cranberry Cake

Norma Keeler ❋ Bear Island

This is a favorite with my sons and grandchildren!

3 eggs
2 cups sugar
1 teaspoon almond extract
¾ cup butter or margarine, cubed
2 cups flour
2½ cups fresh or frozen cranberries
⅔ cup chopped pecans

Preheat oven to 350°F. Grease and flour a 13x9-inch baking pan.
Beat eggs and sugar together for 5 minutes.
Add almond extract and cubed butter. Beat an additional 2 minutes.
Stir in flour, cranberries and nuts.
Spread into prepared pan.
Bake 45 to 50 minutes or until top is light brown.

Fresh Apple Cake

Susan MacBride ❋ Welch Island

1 cup packed brown sugar
1 cup granulated sugar
¼ teaspoon salt
¼ teaspoon nutmeg
2 teaspoons cinnamon
1 teaspoon allspice
1⅛ cup canola oil
2 eggs
2 teaspoons vanilla
2 teaspoons baking soda
2 teaspoons lemon juice
3 cups flour
3 cups chopped apples, peeled and cored
1 cup walnuts, finely chopped

Preheat oven to 350°F. Butter and flour a 13x9-inch baking pan.
Mix together the sugars, salt, spices and oil. To this, add eggs and vanilla.
Sprinkle soda on top of batter. To activate, pour lemon juice on top of soda.
The batter will be very heavy – beat well with an electric mixer.
By hand, stir in flour, apples and nuts. Stir until ingredients are incorporated.
Spread cake batter into prepared baking pan.
Bake for 45-60 minutes or until toothpick comes out clean.
Be careful not to over bake.
Great as is, but also good with Maple Cream frosting.

Maple Cream Frosting

Island ❋ Basics

1 (8-ounce) package cream cheese, softened
¼ cup unsalted butter, room temperature
1 cup Confectioners' sugar
2 tablespoons maple syrup
¼ teaspoon maple-flavored extract

Using a mixer beat all the ingredients on medium until fluffy.
Spread frosting evenly over cooled cake.

July 4th Anniversary Cake

Barbara Whetstone ✻ Treasure Island

We have made this cake for 25 years with the same 6 families. Sometimes we have added sparklers and even Gnomes when they were popular.

2 (18.25-ounce) packages lemon cake mix
1 (12-ounce) small jar apricot jam
Eggs, oil and water (per package directions)
2 pints whipping cream
1 teaspoon vanilla
Confectioners' sugar, to taste
3 snack-size containers vanilla pudding
2 quarts strawberries, halved
2 quarts blueberries
1 quart grapes, halved
6 kiwis, peeled and sliced

Prepare cakes as directed *except add the jam to the batter.* Pour batter into 2 large sheet cake pans and bake according to package directions. Remove from oven and cool completely.

For assembly, spread the pudding on the bottom layer and arrange the kiwi and grapes on top of the pudding.

Place the second sheet cake on top of the first and frost with whipped cream. Decorate the top of cake with the remaining fruit, creating an American flag with the strawberries and blueberries.

✻ ✻ ✻ ✻ ✻

WHAT DO YOU SAY WHEN YOU SEE THE MOUNT?

The Mount Washington Cruise Ship is an icon of Lake Winnipesaukee. For years, our families and friends have played a similar game of "Calling It" when someone catches sight of the Mount, cruising in the distance. This amounts to nothing more than personal satisfaction, but none the less, it tends to be a very competitive game. The calls that we know are: "Spotted It", "First to see the Mount" and "Hosie. I got it."

Kahlua Cake

Nancy McNitt ✳ Spider Island

1 (18.25-ounce) package dark fudge cake mix
2 cups sour cream
1 (3.4-ounce) package instant vanilla pudding
2 eggs
½ cup canola or vegetable oil
½ cup *Kahlua*
1 (12-ounce) package chocolate chips
Confectioners' sugar for garnish

Preheat oven to 350°F. Grease and flour a Bundt pan or spring form pan.

Mix together cake mix, sour cream, instant pudding, eggs, oil and *Kahlua*. When batter is well mixed, fold in the chocolate chips.

Bake 45-50 minutes. (Do not overcook or cake will be dry.) Remove from oven. Allow to cool 10 minutes before inverting onto a serving plate.

Sprinkle with Confectioners' sugar.
Serve with your choice of ice cream and/or hot fudge sauce.

Harold Dexter at the Helm
Photo Courtesy of Mary Dexter

Deep Cove Blueberry Pie

Sharon Doyle ✳ Bear Island

This is Anne Brenner's blueberry pie recipe.

2 tablespoons flour
¾ cup sugar
¼ teaspoon salt
½ teaspoon cinnamon
Juice of ¼ lemon
3 cups of fresh blueberries (handpicked, if possible)
2 tablespoons butter, melted
Pie dough for 2-crust pie

Preheat oven to 450°F. Mix together flour, sugar, salt and cinnamon.

Squeeze lemon juice over blueberries. Toss blueberries in melted butter until coated. Gently blend with flour mixture until evenly mixed and berries are coated.

Line a pie plate with pastry. Pierce with fork. Pour blueberry mixture into pie shell, mounding them at the center. Put on the top crust. Press the edges to seal then pierce to vent.

Bake about 40 minutes. If top crust starts to brown too quickly, cover lightly with sheet of foil or brown paper.

DEEP COVE PARTIES
Bear Island - Sharon Doyle

My parents and their friends were all World War II veterans and they loved to have a good party, especially on the 4th of July.

Entertainment was provided by the younger kids and the ancient piano which still sits in our living room. A full dinner was served to go along with the drinks.

Here is the menu for the party in 1956:
Cheese and Crackers
Homemade Pizza (Rosie Taranto)
Lobster Thermidor (Kay Sauerbrunn)
Garlic Bread
Salad
Blueberry Pie (Anne Brenner)

Toll House Blueberry Pie

Norma Keeler ❋ Bear Island

This is my mother's blueberry pie recipe.

1 cup fresh blueberries
1 cup water
¾ cup sugar or ½ cup *Splenda*
1 tablespoon cornstarch

3-4 cups fresh blueberries
1 baked pie shell

Combine water with 1 cup fresh blueberries and sugar.
Cook until sugar is melted.

In a cup, blend 1 tablespoon of cold water into the cornstarch.
Pour cornstarch mixture into the hot blueberry mixture and cook until thickened.

In a bowl, combine fresh berries with the cooked blueberry mixture, tossing to coat. Pour filling into the baked pie shell.
Cover and refrigerate for several hours.

Serve with whipped cream.

How to Freeze Your Own Blueberries

After you have picked your blueberries, lay them out on a cookie sheet and pick out all the leaves, stems, spiders, webs and un-ripened berries... basically anything unappetizing.

The secret to successful freezing is to package berries **unwashed** *and completely dry.*

Store berries in either resealable plastic bags or air-tight plastic containers.
If you wish, arrange dry berries in a single layer on a cookie sheet and freeze. When frozen, transfer berries to plastic bags or freezer containers.

No~Bake Lemon Pie

Lisa Harris ❋ Mink Island

*Believe it or not, as easy as this is, my mother won a cooking
contest with this pie years ago because it is so yummy!*

1 (14~ounce) can sweetened condensed milk
1 (6~ounce) can frozen lemonade
1 (8~ounce) container *Cool Whip*
6-8 tablespoons fresh lemon juice
1 (10-inch) graham cracker pie crust
Shaved chocolate pieces

In a mixing bowl combine sweetened condensed milk, lemonade and *Cool Whip*. Blend thoroughly. Stir in lemon juice.

Pour filling into graham cracker crust.
Cover and freeze until very firm.

Sprinkle with shaved chocolate pieces before serving.

Variation:
*This pie is delicious as-is, but if you have a big crowd coming and need to stretch this recipe
into two pies, that can be done simply by adding additional ingredients:*

1 (8~ounce) package cream cheese, softened
1 (8~ounce) can crushed pineapple, drained

2 (9~inch) graham cracker pie crusts

Blend the cream cheese in with the lemonade mixture, beating until smooth.
Fold the pineapple in with the lemon juice.
And voila… you have two 9-inch pies instead of one 10-inch.

These additions make the pie a little denser and give it a tropical feel with the
addition of the pineapple.

Tup's Frozen Key Lime Pie

Goodhue Family ❊ Mark Island

¾ cup real lime juice
1 (14-ounce) can sweetened condensed milk
1 (3-ounce) package cream cheese, softened
1 teaspoon freshly grated ginger root
4 tablespoons grated lime zest

1 pint whipping cream
¼ cup sugar
1 (10-inch) graham cracker pie crust

In a large mixing bowl, combine lime juice, sweetened condensed milk, cream cheese, ginger root and lime zest.
Beat until smooth.

In a separate bowl, beat together whipping cream and sugar until cream is thick and forms stiff peaks. Fold whipped cream into flavored cream cheese mixture until well incorporated.

Pour filling into prepared pie crust. Cover and freeze.
Remove from freezer, allowing pie to soften 5–10 minutes before serving.
Garnish with a dollop of whipped cream and a slice of lime.

Tup Goodhue, Gretchen Shortway, Brad Thompson
Waterski Champs

Key Lime Pie

Jim Wells ❊ Mark Island

You will have to snitch the graham crackers,
which were probably destined for Kelsie Grant's S'mores!

Crust:
4½ tablespoons butter, melted
20 graham crackers, (⅓ of box)
¼ cup of sugar
1 teaspoon cinnamon, optional

Filling:
3 egg yolks
1 (14-ounce) can sweetened condensed milk
½ cup Key Lime juice (more if you like it tart)

Preheat oven to 375°F.

Crust:
While butter is melting, seal the graham crackers in a resealable plastic bag.
Crush crackers and roll them to crumbs with a rolling pin or a wine bottle.
In a mixing bowl, combine graham cracker crumbs, sugar and cinnamon; add melted butter. Stir to combine.
Using the back of a spoon, press crumbs into a 9-inch pie plate to form crust.
Bake for 12 minutes. Cool completely.

Filling:
In a mixing bowl, thoroughly whisk together egg yolks, sweetened condensed milk and lime juice. Pour filling into prepared crust.
Bake at 350° for 15 minutes. Cool completely, then refrigerate until ready to serve.

Note: Key Lime juice is often found in the bar/mix section of the grocery store.

Crumb Crust

Island ✴ Basics

Simple to make and ample enough to line larger pies (10-inch) or for recipes using a spring-form pan. Try swapping the graham crackers for your favorite cookies.

½ cup butter (1 stick)
1½ cups graham cracker crumbs (or cookie crumbs)
⅓ cup Confectioners' sugar (regular sugar may be substituted)

Melt butter. Mix in crumbs and sugar. Pour mixture into a pie plate or spring-form pan and press crumbs firmly in bottom and up sides.
Chill 1 hour before filling or bake at 350°F. for 8 minutes.
Cool, chill, and fill.

Frozen Chocolate Amaretto Pie

Priscilla Mayo Sutcliffe ✴ Lockes Island

Our family enjoys this pie year-round, but it is especially easy to prepare in the summer months at the lake. We all know getting frozen foods to the island can be a challenge, so bring your cooler to the market. No matter where I make this pie, people are sure that I have slaved to create this masterpiece.

1 store-bought chocolate graham cracker pie crust
1 half-gallon chocolate ice cream or frozen yogurt
½ – ¾ cup sliced almonds
3 tablespoons of Amaretto (*Disaronno* preferred)

Freeze the pie shell (right in the packaging is okay).
Scoop out ¾ of the container of ice cream and soften in a large bowl.

Set oven to 350°F. Keeping a close eye on them, *gently* toast the almond slices on a baking sheet for a few minutes.

Blend softened ice cream and amaretto together with an electric mixer.
Transfer filling to frozen pie shell.

Sprinkle almonds over the top of filling. Cover and freeze for several hours.

Snickers Pie

Kathleen Aceto ❋ Welch Island

Feel free to play around with different flavors of ice cream, cookies or candy bars, but this is our most requested dessert.

1 gallon vanilla ice cream
1 (1.2-pound) bag *Oreo* cookies
3 tablespoons melted butter
6 *Snickers* candy bars, cut into small pieces

Scoop ice cream into large bowl. Allow to soften.

Place Oreos in a plastic bag and crush using a rolling pin. Add melted butter to the plastic bag and reseal. Work the contents of the bag with your hands until butter is evenly distributed through the cookie crumbs.

Pour crumb mixture into a buttered springform pan. Press crumbs to form a crust on the bottom and sides of pan.

Add *Snickers* pieces to partially melted ice cream and stir until mixed. Spoon filling into prepared cookie crust. Cover and freeze.

4~Minute Brownie Pie

Mary Beth Clason ❋ Diamond Island

Great while playing those late night board and card games.

2 eggs
1 cup sugar
½ cup butter, softened
½ cup flour
4 tablespoons unsweetened cocoa powder
1 teaspoon vanilla
1 teaspoon salt

Preheat oven to 325°F. Butter an 8-inch pie plate.

In a mixing bowl, beat eggs, sugar, butter, flour, cocoa powder, vanilla and salt together until smooth. Spread batter into prepared pie plate.

Bake for 30 minutes. Serve as is or with your favorite topping.

Brad Thompson   Photo Courtesy of Joel Foderberg

Down East Welch Island Lobster Bake

Kettle Grill Roasted Turkey

Kettle Grill Roasted Rib Roast

Pocket Stew

Kielbasa Veggie Grill

Bean Hole Baked Beans

Mark Island Bean Hole Beans

Dough Boys

Down East Welch Island Lobster Bake

Brad Thompson ✳ Welch Island

I need to begin with crediting an old salty buddy of mine – "Seaweed Steve" for introducing me to the Welch Isle technique of a lobster bake. "The Weed" put on many great bakes for decades, but now has slowed to a crawl.

Because of the effort required, I'd say the minimum attendees at a now-famous Welch Island Lobster Bake, should be at least 25. The maximum for a full bake on one pit is probably about 60 (a stuffed box). You can certainly increase the number with a second box.

There are specifics to a successful bake. The correct equipment, best quality ingredients and the proper cooking technique must be closely followed. I will refer to the sketch on the next page during this description.

The sketch details:

- Stacked cement blocks
- 1 (3' 6" x 4'0") ⅜" steel plate with continuous 2" x 2" welded angle-iron
- 1 (3' x 3' 6" x 18" high) plywood box with ¼" x ¼" wire mesh on the bottom

The box must be very rugged as a full 60-person bake will weigh 100-120 pounds.

Other than the food, other items required are:

- 6-8 armfuls of softwood dry slabs*, 3'-4' long
- 3 garbage bags of seaweed (75-pounds)
- An operational garden hose
- 1 piece of cloth canvas about 6' x 12' (without holes)
- 4 pairs of waterproof gloves
- A rake and a shovel
- Two 5-pound cheese cloth, onion or mesh bags

An important engineering detail is that the cement blocks must be set up so that the top of the blocks are perfectly level. If not, then the 1½" of water in the steel plate will vary and the cooking will not occur consistently throughout.

*Slab wood/softwood is important, as it burns hot and quick…broken down pallets would work.

Drawing of Lobster Pit Construction

By Brad Thompson ❄ Welch Island

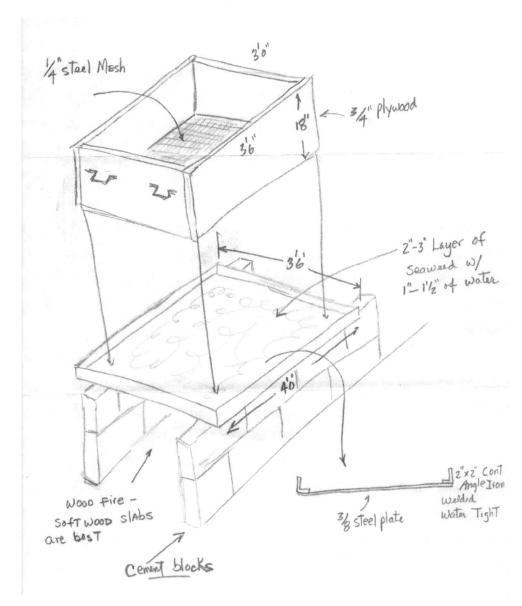

¼" steel Mesh

3'0"

18"

¾" plywood

3'6"

2"-3" Layer of Seaweed w/ 1"-1½" of water

3'6"

4'0"

2"x2" Cont Angle Iron Welded Water TighT

Wood Fire – SofT wood slabs are besT

⅜ steel plate

Cement blocks

Start a good hot fire about one hour and 15 minutes before your planned sit-down. Once the fire is going, place a 2" thick layer of seaweed on the steel pan, and then place the steel pan on top of the pit. Fill the pan with water. You must tend the fire to the point of being sure there is constantly at least 1" of water in the steel pan. If it burns out and evaporates, you will have an awful mess and a lot of hungry people!

Down East Welch Island Lobster Bake (continued)

If you are planning a "bake" for 35 people and we assume they all want a lobster, here's the shopping list:

35 medium potatoes
35 ears of corn
10 lbs. of Steamers
*40 lobsters

*Someone always wants a second lobster or unexpected guests stop by – smelling the bake. There'll be potatoes and corn left over.

Packing the Box:
1. Place a 2" layer of seaweed on the steel pan.
2. Place a 3" layer of seaweed in the bottom of the box.
3. Place the steamers in two 5-pound cheese cloth, onion or mesh bags.
4. Randomly layer all ingredients on top of each other—the corn (remove all but one layer of husk), the lobsters, the potatoes (loose, not wrapped), and the steamers (in bags).
5. As you stack the food, be sure to pack a 1" layer of seaweed up the side of the box.
6. Take one medium-size potato, place it in a piece of cheese cloth and tie a 3' piece of rope to it. This is the *test* potato. This potato should be placed near the top and middle of the pile of food so you can retrieve it easily.
7. Place a generous layer of seaweed over the top of the food.
8. Fold the canvas in half so you have a 6' x 6' cover. Place the canvas over the box and tuck all edges well down in-between the inside of the plywood box and the seaweed which comes up the side of the box.

Once the water in the steel pan is boiling, find four strong people to lift the box over the fire and onto the plate. CAUTION: This needs to be talked about and planned out, as you've got one chance to do it. No bare feet. You're dealing with boiling water and a lot of heat near your feet.

Check your watch. In 50 minutes you should remove the *test* potato and check it. It should be soft and ready to serve. That is your signal that the whole bake is 5-10 minutes away from being ready – no more.

Now reverse your steps. Again, you'll need a 4-person crew to lift the box and move it some place stable, away from the fire. Remove the canvas to stop the cooking. USE CAUTION: the canvas has kept the steam in the food.
The excess steam billows out from the bottom of the box.

Carefully remove the lobsters, potatoes, corn, and steamers—all done to perfection and ready to eat. Don't forget to add butter to the shopping list!

Kettle Grill Roasted Turkey

Brian and Debbie Buell Carroll ❈ Mark Island

The secret to this delicious turkey is in the bacon basting!

1 (15-pound) Turkey (or whatever size meets your needs)
Salt and pepper
1 pound sliced bacon
Charcoal
Foil drip pan, 6x12x1½-inches (can be made from a double thickness of aluminum foil)

Unwrap the turkey and remove the gizzard package from the cavity.
Thoroughly wash the turkey inside and out.
Season turkey with salt and pepper.

On the lower rack in the kettle grill, place the drip pan in the center.
Stack 25-30 charcoal briquettes on each side of the drip pan. Light both piles of charcoal. When you are certain that the charcoal is well lit and the briquettes have started to turn grey around the edges, set the grilling rack in place, with handle opening over the charcoal fires, so you can add more briquettes each hour.

Place the turkey in a roasting rack on center of the grill, over the drip pan.
Cover the turkey with strips of bacon; then cover with aluminum foil.
Place the domed lid on the grill and adjust the vent to keep the fires burning.
After 1 to 1½ hours, remove the domed cover and add more charcoal.
At this point, remove the foil to allow the bacon to crisp.
Replace the domed lid.
Check in a few minutes and once the bacon is crisp, remove the cooked bacon and replace it with the rest of the raw bacon.
Cover the grill and continue to cook. (*This is when every one present hovers around the grill in hopes of scoring a slice of smoked, turkey-flavored bacon. It's delicious with beer!*)
Keep an eye on the turkey and the second batch of bacon.
Turkey is done when the thermometer pops up or the internal temperature reaches 180° in the thigh.

Remove the turkey from the grill and cover with foil.
Allow to rest for 20 minutes before carving.

Serves 6-8 with your favorite accompaniments.

Kielbasa Veggie Grill

Martina Howe ❄ Chip Island

Adjust quantities for the number of mouths you are feeding!

Kielbasa, sliced
Onions, chopped
Mushrooms, sliced
Green beans, ends snipped
Summer squash, sliced
Zucchini, sliced
Red peppers, sliced
Potatoes, cubed
Garlic, grated
Rosemary, chopped

Place any or all of the above ingredients on a large sheet of heavy-duty aluminum foil. Drizzle with New Hampshire maple syrup. Seal as tightly as possible. (Make individual packets, if you wish.)

Place on grill over low flame. Shake occasionally to spread juices around.
Cook until the potatoes are tender, 45 – 50 minutes.

Enjoy your favorite margaritas while you wait!

Note: This can also be cooked over campfire coals.

❄ ❄ ❄ ❄ ❄

Thursday Evening J-80 Races

Our camp is tucked into the woods on Cow Island, facing westerly towards Ragged Island. It is a small A-frame that we built about 14 years ago and we love every minute we can spend out there. Each evening around dusk our family and often some of our neighbors in the cove, our cat and 3 dogs, like to go out on the deck to watch "the squirrel channel."

We have suet and a block of seeds hung in our trees right next to the deck, which feed various island birds (nuthatches, blue jays, woodpeckers) during the day. At night up to a dozen flying squirrels come in to enjoy the feast. We hear them coming towards us through the woods, making their high-pitched "peeping" noises. They arrive with a swoosh, sometimes almost dive-bombing our heads and creating a lot of interest from our cat and dogs, who sit quietly in rapt attention, watching these cute, soft, grey, tiny squirrels with huge black eyes run up and down our trees! It is the best entertainment on the island and better than any nature channel on TV.

The Squirrel Channel
Photo Courtesy of Muriel Robinette

Bean Hole Baked Beans

Jim Wells ✳ Mark Island

Chapter 1: Constructing the Bean Hole

Get your cast-iron or fired-clay bean pot. Dig a hole 4 times as wide and 3 times as deep as your pot. On the bottom, put a large stone with the flat side level and up. Build a circular rock wall back up to ground level, leaving enough room to easily hold your bean pot. *Hint: large rocks hold heat longer.* Back-fill as you build, with compact soil, small rocks, or sand – not the combustible surface stuff. Make the top rim as level as feasible, so the cover will lie flat.

The cover must be large enough to bridge the stone edges. A large flat stone, metal plate or wood cover will do. (Mine is two old pieces of ¾ inch plywood screwed together.) Wood insulates better than metal.
Note: The beans are unaffected by either a square or round cover.

Chapter 2: Firing and Cooking

Light a wood fire in the pit, and burn until the soot which is formed, burns off the rocks—and they appear white. Allow at least a couple of hours for this to happen.

Remove any large burning wood from the hole to a safe place. Part the coals and lower the bean pot so it is level. Quickly, put the cover over the hole and seal the edges with damp wood chips, damp sand, damp leaves, an old canvas, or whatever. If the cover is metal, insulate the whole top with the chosen sealing material. Cover smoke-holes as they appear. The coals will suffocate after awhile. That's okay; it's the heated rocks that do the baking.
Beans in the hole by 10 o'clock in the morning will be ready for supper.

When it's time to eat, tip the bean hole cover aside and extract the bean pot.
Dust ash and debris off the cover before opening. A tight-fitting cover may be stuck on from some of the initial boil-over. The bottom of the bean pot may be hot and messy. Have an old, driftwood board ready, rather than your camp's heirloom trivet.

Bean Hole Baked Beans continued on next page…

Bean Hole Baked Beans continued:

<u>Chapter 3: Vegetarian Baked Beans</u> (wife doesn't eat meat)

> For 8-10 people (with leftovers for cold, baked bean sandwiches)
> Fits into standard size, cast-iron covered baking pot

3 pounds dry beans (a mix of 3 kinds, such as navy pea, Jacob's cattle, soldier, or yellow-eye)
1 tablespoon salt, divided
1 (12-ounce) beer
2 tablespoons dry mustard
½ cup vinegar
¾ cup dark brown sugar
¾ cup molasses
¾ cup chopped onion
1 quartered onion
2 garlic cloves
6 tablespoons butter

> For more than 10 people
> Fits in a 12-quart bean pot

5 pounds dry beans (a mix of 3 kinds)
2 tablespoons salt, divided
1 (12-ounce) beer
¼ cup dry mustard
¾ cup vinegar
1¼ cup dark brown sugar
1¼ cup molasses
1 cup chopped onion
1-2 quartered onion
3 garlic cloves
8 tablespoons butter

<u>Directions:</u>
The night before: Pick over the beans to make sure there are no pebbles or ugly looking rejects (shriveled black things). Cover the beans in water; add half the salt and soak over night.

The next day: Drain water and discard. Add beer to the drained beans and then add enough fresh water to cover.
Bring beans and liquid to a boil, then reduce to a simmer for about 1 hour or until skins wrinkle when blown on. Drain liquid and reserve. Combine the dry mustard, vinegar, brown sugar, molasses, chopped onion, and the other half of the salt with a pint (or so) of the reserved liquid.

Grease the bean pot. Dump the beans into the pot. Pour the above combined mixture over the beans. Top with quartered onions, garlic cloves, and butter.

Before lowering the bean pot into the bean hole, top off with remaining reserved liquid (and if necessary, more warm water) to fill the pot.
Put on the cover and lower it into the bean hole (see Chapter 2).

Jim Wells Tending the Bean Hole   Photo Courtesy of Cyrene Wells

GOOD MEMORIES
Sleepers Island – Tim and Joanne Moulton

We purchased our land on Sleepers Island in 1966. My husband and I built our island chalet on weekends and our Massachusetts home during the week.
Yes! We have had more than 40 years on this precious lake.

We used to come to the island for February vacations. I planned most meals ahead and we heated them on the stove. All water systems were drained for the winter, so we carried water from an ice-hole when needed. The children slid on plastic sleds and we ice-skated around the island. Good memories. We had ice so thick we drove our Volvo to the dock. Many supplies were brought on sleds also.

Our family cooked on a wood fire for over 30 years. A social hour was held on the dock, while dinner cooked: grilled fish, chicken, steak, kabobs, potatoes quartered with cheese and bacon and herbs, wrapped in foil on fire, corn (silk removed, husks on, dipped in water) placed on a grill or fire, turned every ten minutes, and S'mores for dessert.

Mark Island Bean Hole Beans

Ray Keating ✳ Mark Island

The Bean Hole

Dig a pit at least 3 feet deep by 3-4 feet diameter (no small task on this island). Our pit was dug with a large buried rock making up one side. Place flat stones level on the bottom of the pit and line the sides of the pit with rocks. You will need some kind of a fireproof cover for the pit, such as a large flat stone or a steel plate. At least 4 to 6 hours before you start cooking the beans, build a fire in the pit. You can use any wood, but hardwood or natural charcoal works the best.

Keep the fire burning until you are ready to start cooking the beans (beans should cook for at least 8 hours). Allow the fire to burn down to coals.

(You will also need a quantity of sand or loose dirt to seal the edges of the cover during cooking.)

The Bean Ingredients:

½ pound each of three (or more) different beans, such as soldier, pinto, Lima, kidney, or black beans. The idea is to create a mixture of beans of various colors and sizes.

1 cup molasses

2 tablespoons ketchup

½ cup brown sugar

1 tablespoon dried mustard or ¼ cup prepared mustard

½ cup vinegar (cider or white)

1-2 cloves garlic, peeled

1 package salt pork

1 pound ground pork

Salt and pepper to taste

1 medium onion, peeled and halved

Preparation:

Mix the selected beans together and soak overnight. In the morning, drain the beans, place them in a cooking kettle, cover with fresh water, and bring them to a boil. Reduce heat and simmer until skins wrinkle when blown on.

Meanwhile, mix the molasses, ketchup, brown sugar, mustard and vinegar in a sauce pan, and cook over medium heat until the sugar is dissolved.

Add whole garlic cloves to the molasses mixture.

Score the salt pork by slicing nearly to the rind in ¼ inch slices.

Sauté the ground pork until lightly browned, breaking into small pieces as it cooks; season with salt and pepper.

When the beans are ready, drain, reserving the cooking water.

Place beans in a bean pot or cast-iron covered pot.

Mark Island Bean Hole Beans (continued)

Mix in the ground pork and the molasses mixture; push the onion and salt pork into the beans.

Add reserved cooking water to just cover beans. If there is insufficient cooking water, add more tap water or a bottle of your favorite island beer.

Shovel out the pit, reserving enough coals to allow you to partially bury the bean pot. Place the cooking pot on the bottom of the pit; bank a few hot coals around the base of the pot.

Put the cover over the pit; shovel sand all around the edges to create a seal for heat retention.

<u>Helpful Hints:</u>

It's a good idea to notify the Gilford Fire Department that you intend to fire up your bean hole, as you probably won't have enough beans left after feeding the crew from Snuffer to feed your family.

Your cooking vessel should have some kind of handle or chain attached to allow you to retrieve the beans without having to reach way down in the pit.

Check the beans once after 2 or 3 hours to see if you have enough liquid. Add more if necessary.

Don't open the pit too often; you lose a lot of heat that way.

✻ ✻ ✻ ✻ ✻

FROM THE BEGINNING
Mark Island - Ray Keating

Chris and I started coming to Mark Island when we met in 1971. Her grandfather had bought 2 island lots in the 1950s, one of which was later owned by her father and the other by her uncle. We tented for a few years and then were able to purchase her uncle's lot and began building our camp.

During most of the 1970s and early 1980s we moved to the island every summer with our five daughters, one dog, two cats and various other pets, including rabbits, gerbils and hamsters.

We've done a lot of cooking on the island and have many fond memories of fun guests and interesting meals.

Dough Boys

Linda Buell Keith ❋ Mark Island

4 campfire sticks, (directions below)
2 cups *Bisquick* baking mix
½ cup water
½ cup strawberry jam

Making the sticks:
Cut green sticks approximately 3-feet long and 1-inch in diameter. Trim the bark off each limb 6-inches up from one end. Hold trimmed end over hot coals to cure, or dry out a bit.

Making the dough:
Combine *Bisquick* and water; using a fork, mix until stiff dough is formed. Form one-forth of dough around each prepared stick, squeezing with your hand to be sure it is secure.

Cook dough boys over moderate campfire coals until lightly brown, rotating frequently. Be careful not to burn. Cool a bit.

Slide dough off stick; fill with 2 tablespoons of jam. Enjoy!

❋ ❋ ❋ ❋ ❋

MARSHMALLOW SKINS
Mark Island - Emily Buell

As a kid, I remember camping on the east side of Mark Island with my entire family. On most camping trips, we would build a fire and of course we'd have to toast marshmallows. Being young, getting the perfect golden brown skin was always a bit difficult; it was so much easier to just stick them in the flames and let them burn. Granted, you must like the taste of a burnt marshmallow! And so began the tradition of burning layer by layer: pulling off the burnt marshmallow skin and eating it, and then re-burning the marshmallow, pulling off the skin again, and repeating this until there was nothing left. Our family began trying to make a record amount of burnt marshmallow layers, and I believe our best still stands at a solid ten!

Nancy and Billy Buell with Nancy Bryant Tenting on Mark Island

Emily Buell with a Perfectly Toasted Marshmallow
Photo Courtesy of Jill Buell

Contributors

There are so many people to thank for contributing to our *Winnipesaukee Cuisine* project. The enthusiastic response was beyond our expectations.

Barndoor Island
 Jenni Gemberling

Bear Island
 Pattie Jean Collins

 Sharon Doyle

 Carmel Hanson

 Norma Keeler

 Harold Lyon

 Suzanne Morrissey

 Renee & Craig Richard

Camp Island
 Bobbe Fairman

 Virginia & Thaddeus Thorne

Chase Island
 Evy Chapman

Cow Island
 Roxane Gwyn

 Anne B. Minkoff

 Muriel & Michael Robinette

Chip Island
 Martina & Andy Howe

Deven's Island
 Brenda Stowe

Diamond Island
 Mary Beth & Kurt Clason

 Nanci Stone

Dolly Island
 Amelia Katzen

Jolly Island
 Estelle Miller

Little Bear Island
 Cheryl Bogardus

 Barbara Cohen

 Lynda & Walter Johnson

 Pattie Bezanson Fielding

 Jeff Hamlin

Little Camp Island
 Ann Beane

Little Goodwin Island
 Maureen Mustapha

Lockes Island
 Margaret Boulas

 Karen & Rick Dean

 Jayne Gray

 Marylou Koning

 Jan & Nelson Maynard

 Dot & Dave Pangburn

 Ruth Stewart

 Priscilla & Peter Sutcliffe

 Carole & Roger Tropf

Loon Island
 The Tower Family

Mark Island
 Mary Anne & Kim Baron

 Jeannette & Bill Buell

 Emily Buell

 Jill Billings Buell

 Nancy L. Buell

 Debbie & Brian Carroll

 Millie & Rusty Elwell

 Glenn Fuller

 Diana & John Goodhue

 Marcia & Tom Haughey

 Laura Jean & Richard &
  Scott & Melinda Holdaway

 Anne A. Hummel

 Christine & Ray Keating

 Brenda Keith

 Linda Buell Keith

 Lisa Rich Libby

 Renate & Dick Marcoux

 Louise & Ted McKean

 Alida Millham

 Jennifer & Jamie Wells

 Cyrene & Jim Wells

 Marnie Wells-White

Melody Island
Maria & Matt Found

Mink Island
Sue & Steve Cutillo

Joanne & Greg Dickinson

Lisa & Trevor Harris

Margy Knox

Jane Veazey-MacFadzen

Joan Veazey

Becky & Peter Wright

Mt Major Island
Anne MacInnis

Pine Island
Connie Delaney

Crane McCune

Karen McCune

Judith Norton

Pitchwood Island
Margaret Smith

Rattlesnake Island
Julie Caouette

Gwen Gulinello

Debbie Kennedy

Jeannie Leach

Mary Jo Ray

Rock Island
Jean & Robert Carbone

Round Island
Robert Ryan

Sleepers Island
Joanne & Tim Moulton
Susan Brewer

Spider Island
Nancy McNitt

Steamboat Island
Carol & Howard Stoner

Stonedam Island
Katherine Rice

Treasure Island
Claudette & Rodney Gammon
Barbara Whetstone

Two Mile Island
Stephanie & Bill Knighton

Welch Island
Kathleen (Murfee) Aceto

Helen Denley

Mary & Harold Dexter

Becky Thompson Doherty

The Fox Family

Connie & Steve & Kelsie Grant

Wendy & Sean Hanley

Carol & Bob Jones

Kitty Leonardson

Susan & Jim MacBride

Thelma & Karl Malafey

Jen Mason Malafey

Jan & Nelson Maynard

Debbie Kelley Milburn

Abby Thompson

Daryl & Brad Thompson

Whortleberry Island
Gail & Jim Pillow

STORIES INDEX

Index

HUNGRY FOR SUMMER

A Unique Collection of Favorite Recipes
From the Island Residents of Lake Winnipesaukee

Please send me _____ copies of Winnipesaukee Cuisine's Hungry For Summer at $23.95 each plus $5.00 priority mail shipping for the first book, $10.00 shipping for up to 5 books.

Name_____
Address_____
City_____State_____Zip Code_____
Email or phone number _____

Please make checks payable to: Winnipesaukee Cuisine.
Mail to: 27 Mark Island, Gilford, N.H. 03249

Inquires: Info@winnicuisine.com
Check us out at: www.winnicuisine.com

HUNGRY FOR SUMMER

A Unique Collection of Favorite Recipes
From the Island Residents of Lake Winnipesaukee

Please send me _____ copies of Winnipesaukee Cuisine's Hungry For Summer at $23.95 each plus $5.00 priority mail shipping for the first book, $10.00 shipping for up to 5 books.

Name_____
Address_____
City_____State_____Zip Code_____
Email or phone number _____

Please make checks payable to: Winnipesaukee Cuisine.
Mail to 27 Mark Island, Gilford, N.H. 03249

Inquires: Info@winnicuisine.com
Check us out at: www.winnicuisine.com

Breinigsville, PA USA
25 May 2010
238687BV00001B/2/P